D1742708

MAKING GIFTS

ANNE HULBERT

B T BATSFORD LIMITED
London and Sydney

© Anne Hulbert 1975

First published 1975
ISBN 0 7134 2948 8

Filmset by
Servis Filmsetting Limited, Manchester
Printed in Great Britain by
Morrison & Gibb Ltd, Edinburgh
for the publishers
B T Batsford Limited
4 Fitzhardinge Street
London W1H 0AH and
23 Cross Street, PO Box 586
Brookvale NSW 2100
Australia

CONTENTS

INTRODUCTION

ACKNOWLEDGMENT

Making and creating with our hands offers a satisfying solution to one of the present-day problems — that of how to use our spare time to best advantage.

Here is a practical and inspiring book full of delightful things to make at home. There are ideas for making presents, or attractive things for the house. There are also many money-saving and money-making ideas for fetes, bazaars and sales of work. Such a selection provides pastimes for all ages; for those with little time to spare; and for those who have more time to indulge in a new interest.

The clear patterns and instructions are easy to follow. No previous experience or know-how in any of these subjects is necessary, and no expensive tools or equipment are needed.

Do be imaginative — try using different colours, textures and materials. The materials and colours given with the instructions need not be adhered to; if you experiment, then others as well as yourself will derive considerable pleasure from your skill and imagination.

All the items in this book are designed by the author, who also made all but two of the samples photographed. The dried flower arrangement (page 32) was created by floral artist Marilyn Hodges. The Tiffany lampshade (page 41) was made up by Dorothy Atkinson. Photographs by John Hunnex.

MAKING PATTERNS

This section applies to pattern-making throughout the book.

Tools and equipment

Large sheets of paper — cheap white drawing paper, brown paper, or ready-marked graph paper (1 square representing 1 in. or 2·5 cm)

Soft pencil, rubber and ruler

Pair of compasses with small pencil (if you have no compass, mark circles round anything from a button to a large plate)

Plenty of thin card for pattern templates

Polycell wallpaper paste, *Gloy* paste, or flour and waste paper

Old scissors for cutting paper and card

Oddments of string and some polythene bags

Grid system and scale used

Most of the patterns given in this book are marked out on squared grids. Each square on each grid represents 1 in. (2·5 cm), and the pattern pieces have to be enlarged to their full size.

Enlarging the patterns

If you use plain paper, you must mark it up into 1 in. (2·5 cm) squares. Your lines must be straight and accurate all over, and the area marked up must be large enough to accommodate the full size pieces of pattern. (Ready-marked graph paper is very much easier.)

Now copy the patterns on to the squared paper from the diagrams given. Work square by square, and mark a pencil dot at each point where a pattern line crosses a grid or graph paper line. Join up all the dots, all round from square to square carefully and with great accuracy. Carelessly drawn diagrams will result in badly-fitting pattern pieces.

When the patterns are completed, paste the enlargements on to thin card. Allow the paste to dry and cut out each piece. Doing this makes firm templates which are easy to mark out on the material. It will also give you sets of patterns which can be used over and over again. Add all the necessary details and important markings to each piece.

Mark a hole in corresponding templates, thread them on to an oddment of string, and tie together. Store in a polythene bag for future use, clearly marked with the name of each design.

Transferring pattern to material

It is wisest always to mark the wrong side of whatever fabric or material you are using. Hold the template down very firmly with one hand, and draw all round the outline. Use a pale crayon for dark materials, and a dark pencil or crayon for pale-coloured materials. Do not use a ballpoint pen, as smudging could ruin the work.

Remember that, when two identical pattern pieces are required and the material has a right and a wrong side, the template must be reversed. After drawing round it once, turn it over completely for marking the second side. It is a help to mark such templates as 'side 1' and 'side 2'.

Altering scale size of given designs

You may feel that some of the things to make in this book are too large, or even too small. It is easy to alter the scale of the grid diagrams. Just assume the squares are 2 in. (5 cm) instead of 1 in. (2·5 cm) for doubling the size of the pattern, or ½ in. (1·3 cm) instead of 1 in (2·5 cm) for halving the size.

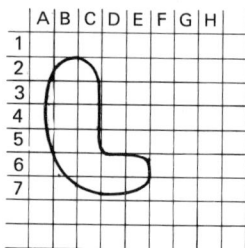
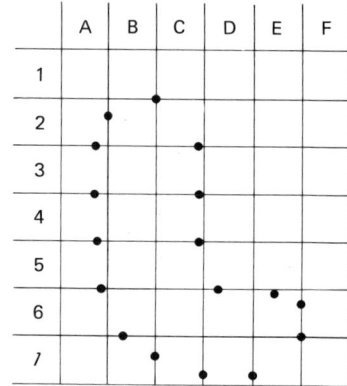
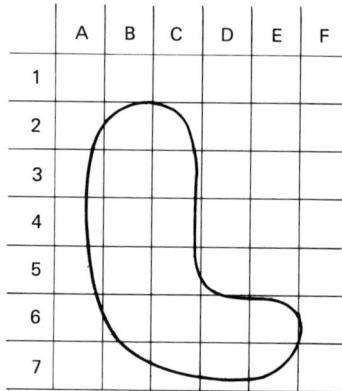

WORKING WITH FABRICS

Introduction

Almost every household has scraps of materials, trimmings, haberdashery and discarded clothes which could be made into something attractive and useful. Remnants of materials are often to be found in shops, and are worth hunting for.

Making something new from bits and pieces is most satisfying, and this Section gives a variety of easy-to-make sewing ideas.

Sewing equipment

Large cutting-out scissors
Small, sharp-pointed scissors

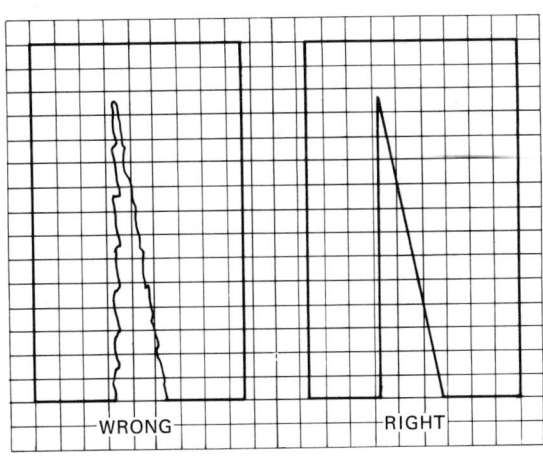

Pinking shears (optional)
Steel pins
Steel needles in various sizes
Tape measure and thimble
Tacking and sewing threads
Iron, ironing board and damp cloth
Sewing machine (not a necessity, but it makes sewing so much quicker)

Any other special materials or equipment needed are indicated in the individual instructions.

Pattern making

This is explained in the previous section, and the same methods apply here.

Cutting out

A wide range of types and textures of materials is available. Some of these necessitate using special techniques when cutting out.

(a) *Felt and PVC* must be cut with a continuous scissor action, since a series of short snips will result in ugly, jagged edges. Felt details must have smooth and straight-cut edges, especially if the stitching is on the right side of the work (see diagram).

(b) *Fur fabric* requires care to avoid cutting through the pile of the fabric, as this results in an unattractive straight and level line of 'fur'. The

9

points of the scissors should be worked between the pile, cutting only the backing. After cutting, the pieces can be eased apart to leave attractive feathery edges to the pile (see diagram).

Always cut out all fabrics carefully, poor cutting can easily spoil a good pattern. Cut right on the marking lines, unless instructed otherwise, and make sure you use very sharp scissors.

The arrows on the pattern pieces show the direction of the fabric grain, and should run parallel to the warp or weft threads of the fabric. When fur fabric or other pile material is used, the arrows indicate the direction in which the pile must run (see diagrams for straight and bias cutting).

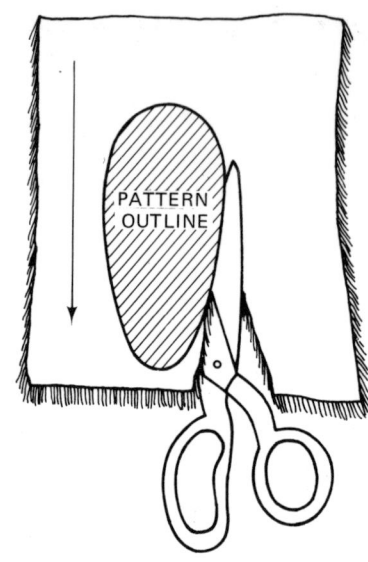

Making up – pinning and tacking

Ideally, the pieces of material should be pinned and tacked together prior to stitching. This ensures that seams come straight, and that the lines of stitching are in the right places. Pinning and tacking is most important if you are to stitch through several thicknesses of fabric; they are then held firmly together and the possibility of them slipping out of position is avoided.

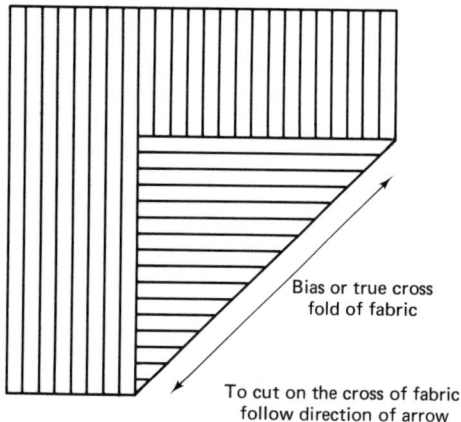

Bias or true cross fold of fabric

To cut on the cross of fabric follow direction of arrow

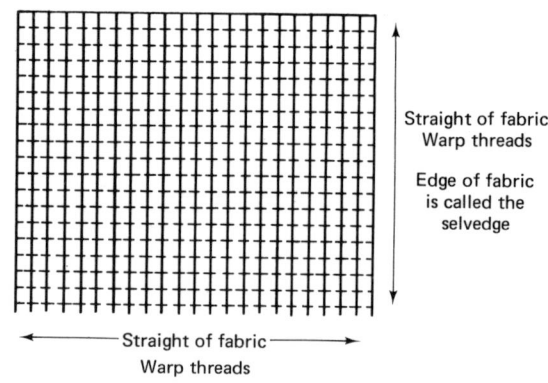

Straight of fabric
Warp threads

Edge of fabric is called the selvedge

Straight of fabric
Warp threads

It is a good idea to use a contrasting colour for the tacking thread — it is easy to see when the time comes to pull it out.

After tacking, do make sure that all pins have been removed.

Stitching

One feels a certain pride in creating something made entirely by hand. However, time is always short, and machine stitching is far quicker. There are some excellent machines to be had which make all sorts of fancy stitches. The manufacturer's handbook will advise on the stitch and thread best suited to the material to be used.

Very fine materials, such as voile and chiffon, are more easily stitched if a layer of tissue paper is laid underneath the fabric and run through the machine with it. Simply tear away the paper afterwards.

Felt generally looks more attractive stitched on the right side of the work, whether you are joining seams or applying pieces of felt to other materials. This top or edge stitching should not be more than $\frac{1}{8}$ in. (3 mm) from the felt edge.

Gluing small pieces of felt in position prior to stitching is highly recommended, especially felt features of toy faces, etc, which need to be firmly applied.

Pressing

Many of us tend to complete our work before pressing any of it, but a more professional finish is achieved if the work is pressed as each step is completed.

If it is necessary to press the right side of the material, use a damp cloth to avoid a shine appearing. Always try the temperature of the iron on a scrap of fabric first, particularly if you are using delicate or man-made fabrics.

Victorian doll nightdress case

See page 20

You will need

9 in. × 15 in. (23 cm × 38 cm) white felt or calico for head and neck
Approx 3 oz (85 g) black rug wool for hair
1 in. × 2 in. (2·5 cm × 5 cm) mauve felt for eyes
1 in. × 1 in. (2·5 cm × 2·5 cm) pink felt for mouth
24 in. × 36 in. (61 cm × 92 cm) printed cotton for dress
22 in. × 36 in. (56 cm × 92 cm) lightweight iron-on *Vilene (Pellon)*
Approx 2½ yd broderie lace for skirt, cuffs and hat frills
Approx ½ yd (46 cm) lace for bib
Approx 7 in. (18 cm) fancy ribbon for bib
6 in. × 8 in. (15 cm × 20 cm) felt for gloves and boots
8 pearl sequins
4½ in. × 30 in. (11 cm × 76 cm) broderie or plain fabric for hat
4 or 5 press studs
Approx ½ lb (227 g) kapok for filling head and boots
Paper for pattern
Copydex
Matching threads

To make

Draw your paper up into 1 in. (2·5 cm) squares, copy the pattern on to it from the diagrams given, and cut out. Cut out all pieces required in fabric and felt.

Head Place both head pieces together with wrong sides facing. Tack and stitch all round, leaving bottom of neck open for turning and filling. Clip round curves and turn to right side.

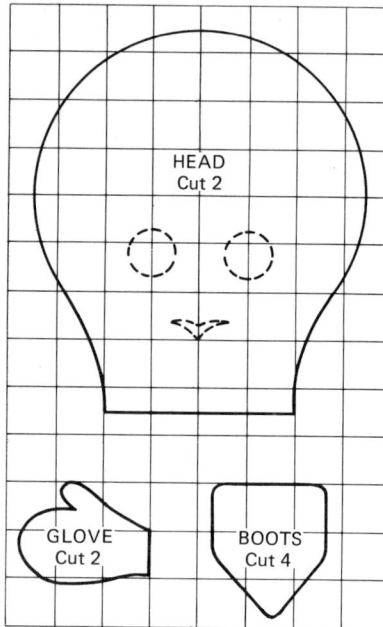

HEAD
Cut 2

GLOVE
Cut 2

BOOTS
Cut 4

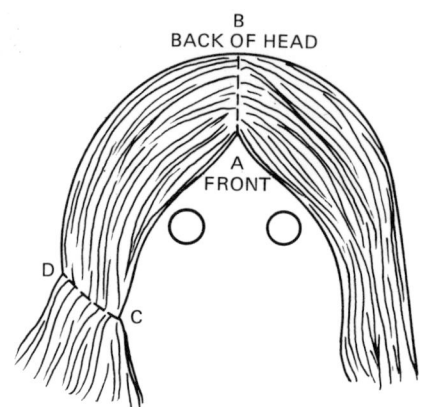

B
BACK OF HEAD

A
FRONT

D

C

Fill with kapok until firm and smooth. Run a gathering thread all round base of neck, turning under ¼ in. (6 mm) as you work. Draw up tight to hold kapok inside, and fasten off securely.

Dress Iron-on *Vilene* is used to give the dress fabric weight and firmness. Out of the printed cotton, cut a strip 2 in. × 10 in. (5 cm × 25 cm) and put aside for the neck band. Cut out the dress piece 22 in. × 36 in. (56 cm × 92 cm), and iron *Vilene* on to the wrong side. Fold the material with right sides facing and meeting the two short ends. Stitch down a few inches (centimetres) from the top and a few inches (centimetres) up from the bottom, leaving a gap large enough to insert nightie or pyjamas through easily. Still working on the wrong side, refold the dress so that the seam falls down the centre of the back. Now stitch across the bottom to

form a bag.

Stitch lace round both sides and one end of fancy ribbon, then stitch completed bib on to the centre front of the dress.

Spread a little *Copydex* on underside of wrist of glove and glue in place on the dress. Cut a 2 in. (5 cm) length of broderie edging, turn the ends under ¼ in. (6 mm), and stitch in place across the wrist. Repeat for other glove.

Run a gathering thread round top edge of dress and pull up to fit the neck of the doll. Pin in place and back stitch firmly all round. Fold the neckband into three lengthways and stitch round the neck to cover raw edges of top of dress. Finish off neatly at the back. Stitch 2 rows of broderie lace along bottom of dress as shown in photograph.

Boots Place 2 boot sections together, wrong sides facing, and stitch all round, leaving straight edges open. Turn to right side and fill softly with kapok. Oversew open end. Stitch 4 sequins down front for buttons. Repeat for other boot. Stitch both boots to seam at bottom of dress.

Hair and face (see diagram) Cut the wool into 36 in. (92 cm) lengths. Spread a thin line of

Copydex along the top of head from back to front. Lay strands of hair across head, pressing them down on glue. Backstitch along centre top of head from back to front (A to B). Catch strands at sides close against neck with a few backstitches from C to D. Divide the loose strands in half, as if to make 2 plaits, and twist each into a coil and pass round towards the back. This will give a side 'bun' effect. Tuck ends under and stitch down. You can of course create your own hair style. If the strands of hair at the sides of the face appear to separate, spread a little glue over side of face and gently press the wool hair down on to it. Glue eyes and mouth in place as shown in pattern, remembering that low-set and wide-apart eyes look younger and prettier.

Hat Fold the 4½ in. × 30 in. (11 cm × 76 cm) fabric in half, meeting the two short ends, with right sides facing. Stitch along to join seam. Run a gathering thread all round one edge, turning under ¼ in. (6 mm) as you work. Pull up as tight as possible to form top of hat. Stitch broderie lacing all round other edge. Run a gathering thread all round bottom, about ¾ in. (19 mm) above edge of lace. Pull this up to fit the doll's head and pin in place with seam at back. Stitch to head at intervals to prevent it falling off.

Sew press studs at about 3 in. (7·6 cm) intervals down the opening at the back of the nightie case.

Lace, sequin and pearl egg cosy

See page 25

A present made from scraps of material, oddments of sequins and pearls, and trimmed with braid. The style can be adapted for use on any flowery lace by just picking out the design in sequins.

You will need

5 in. × 12 in. (13 cm × 30 cm) white lace for outer cover
5 in. × 12 in. (13 cm × 30 cm) bright silk for inner cover
4½ in. × 11 in. (11 cm × 28 cm) felt for lining
12 in. (30 cm) length fringe for trimming
Oddments of sequins and pearl beads
Matching threads
Paper for patterns

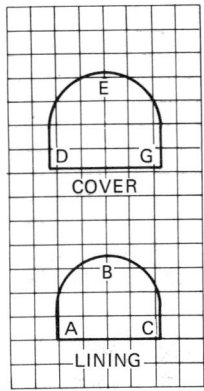

Pattern

Each square = 1 in. (2·5 cm).
Mark your paper up into 1 in. (2·5 cm) squares and copy the pattern on to it from the diagram given. Cut out in paper.

Making up

Outer cover

(¼ in. (6 mm) seams are allowed)
Cut out 2 outer covers in white lace, 2 inner covers in bright silk, and 2 linings in felt. Place

13

one lace piece wrong side down on to right side of one silk piece and tack together all round. Plan your design for working. Stitch sequins and pearls in place, one stitch through each is sufficient. Work on right side of lace and take stitches through to back of silk. Repeat for other side of cosy. With right sides facing, stitch the worked sections together all round, leaving bottom open. Turn to right side.

Lining Stitch the 2 felt pieces together all round with right sides facing, leaving bottom open. Do not turn right side out. Ease lining up inside cosy and oversew all round bottom to lace/silk edges. Stitch fringe all round top of cosy, finishing the ends neatly. Stitch a single row of sequins all round bottom to cover oversewing stitches.

Man's print tie

See page 24

You will need

$13\frac{1}{2}$ in. × 30 in. (34 cm × 76 cm) printed fabric
8 in. × 30 in. (20 cm × 76 cm) soft iron-on
  Vilene (Pellon)
Matching threads
Paper for pattern

To make (pattern: each square equals 1 in. (2·5 cm)

Mark your paper up into 1 in. (2·5 cm) squares and copy the pattern on to it from the diagram given. Cut out all pieces.

Cut out in cotton and *Vilene*. With right sides facing, stitch cotton pieces together from A to B. Press seam open flat. Stitch *Vilene* sections together from A to B.

Matching centre back seams, carefully place

complete *Vilene* interfacing down the centre of wrong side of cotton section, and iron together. Fold one long edge of cotton over on to *Vilene* at the back, overlapping centre line. Catch stitch, by hand, along centre. Avoid the stitches coming through to the front of the tie.

Fold the other edge of cotton over on to *Vilene*, turn under $\frac{1}{4}$ in. (6 mm) all along, and hem to existing line of catch stitches, down the centre.

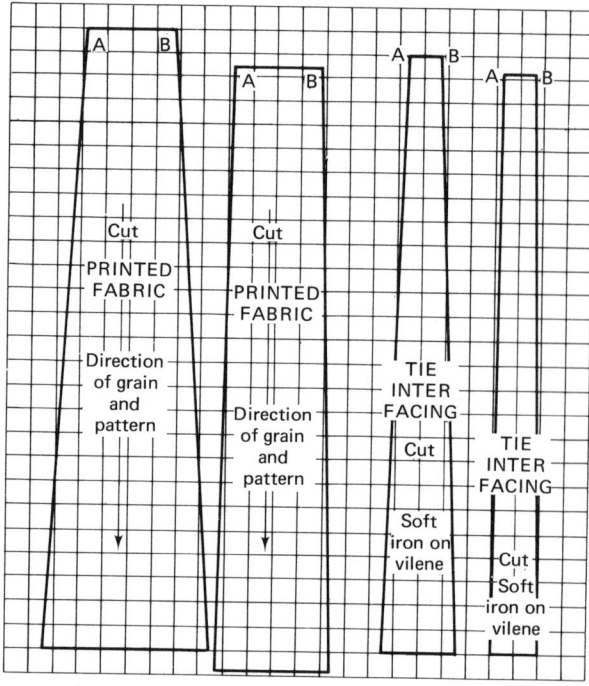

Fold the raw edge at bottom front up inside the tie for about $\frac{1}{2}$ in. (13 mm), and secure with 2 or 3 stitches which cannot be seen. Make sure the bottom is straight, and the corners are square. Repeat for the other end of tie.

Press finished tie carefully.

Fabric tray holder

Useful for keeping trays tidy and out of the way when not in use.

See page 24

You will need

1 wooden curtain ring approx 1½ in (3·8 cm) inside diameter
2 strips of firm cotton, each 42 in. long × 4 in. wide (107 cm × 10 cm)

To make

Fold one piece of fabric lengthways, with right sides facing. Stitch long edges together. Turn to right side. Pass strap through the ring and join ends neatly. Repeat for the second strap. When both straps are through the ring, stitch through both thicknesses of each one, very close to the ring to prevent them from sliding round too easily.

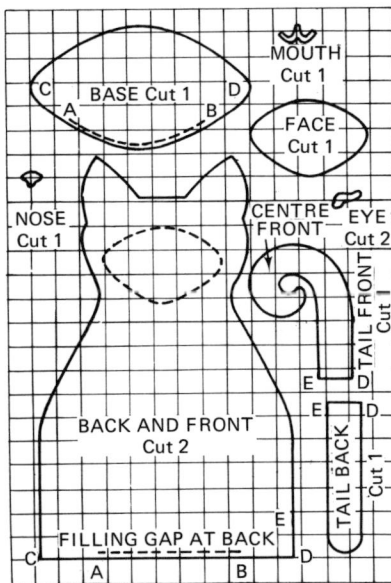

Large cat doorstop

See page 73

This contended cat is a super doorstop. She is easy to make, and will grace any room, sitting quietly where she is put.

You will need

19 in. × 24 in. (48 cm × 62 cm) printed cotton for body
4 in. × 5½ in. (10 cm × 14 cm) white felt for face
5 in. × 6½ in. (13 cm × 16 cm) orange felt for eyes, tail and mouth
1 in. × 1¼ in. (2·5 cm × 3·2 cm) yellow felt for nose
Scraps of wool for whiskers
Approx 10 oz (283 g) kapok for filling
4 lb (1·814 kg) sand for weighting (make sure it is thoroughly clean and dry)
Copydex
Matching threads
Paper for patterns
Strong polythene bag, approx 7 in. × 8 in. (18 cm × 20 cm)

Making up

Scale 1 square represents 1 in. (2·5 cm).

Mark your paper up into 1 in. (2·5 cm) squares, copy the patterns on to it from the diagrams given, and cut out all parts. From the printed cotton and felt, cut out all pieces required.

With right sides facing, stitch back and front together from D at bottom, round ears, and down to C at bottom on other side. Stitch in base, matching CC and DD, leaving gap open from A to B for filling, at back of seam. Clip at curves and corners.

Turn right side out, easing the seams out to a good shape. Stuff with kapok, pushing it well into points of ears, until toy is very firm. Continue stuffing until about three-quarters of the way down the fat part of the body. Fill the polythene bag with sand, seal the bag, and place it in the cat. Surround the bag with kapok and continue filling until full. Stitch up opening and brush off excess kapok.

Face Make complete face before attaching to the head. Using only a little *Copydex*, glue the eyes, nose and mouth on to the face piece, using the photograph as a guide. Stitch all round eyes and nose, but only one line of stitching along mouth.

Work whiskers with wool, making two long stitches of about 2 in. (5 cm) in length on each side. Spread *Copydex* thinly all over back of face and glue to head, then sew all round edge.

Tail Join both tail pieces together from D to E. Spread a thin layer of *Copydex* on the back of the complete tail and glue to body, matching DD at lower side and also the centre front. Stitch all round.

When all work is finished, flatten the base of the cat by slapping it, so that she will stand firmly.

Shiny plastic tote bag

See page 65

You will need

18 in. × 24 in. (46 cm × 62 cm) red shiny PVC

18 in. × 24 in. (46 cm × 62 cm) blue shiny PVC
Gilt rings approx 2 in. (5 cm) in diameter
Eyelet tool kit (there are 4 or 5 brands available in haberdashery departments and include good instructions
Sewing threads
Copydex
Approx 10 paper clips (to hold work in place. Do not use pins)

To make

($\frac{1}{2}$ in. (13 mm) turnings are allowed for throughout.
From the blue PVC cut out as follows:

1 piece 16 in. × 17$\frac{1}{2}$ in. (40 cm × 44 cm) for blue side of bag
1 piece 2 in. × 16 in. (5 cm × 40 cm) for handle
2 pieces 2 in. × 2$\frac{1}{2}$ in. (5 cm × 6·3 cm) for handle tabs

From the red PVC cut exactly the same again, to exactly the same sizes.

Make sure you cut the lines straight everywhere.

Woolly owl; fringed suede pencil holder; frog bean bag

Place one 16 in. (40 cm) end of one of each red and blue section together with right sides facing and stitch along, using a largish stitch. Turn to right side and open the seam flat. Top stitch down each side of seam on the right side of the material. Join together the other 16 in. (40 cm) ends of red and blue pieces in the same way to form a 'tube'. Turn the bag inside out and fold it so that each seam meets, absolutely centrally, at top and bottom of work. Use paperclips to hold it all in position, and stitch along one open end (the bottom of the bag), keeping centre joins matched.

Turn bag to right side and ease out corners squarely. Turn under 1 in (2·5 cm) all round top of bag, and glue down. Stitch all round edge. *Handles* Take a blue handle tab and spread the entire back with *Copydex*. Leave to dry. Fold under ½ in. (13 mm) down each side of the longer edge to meet in the middle at the back. Press down well. (The tab should now be double and 1 in. (2·5 cm) wide by 2½ in. (6·3 cm) long). Pass tab through the ring and meet the ends together. Glue them to stay joined. Now glue this blue tab on to the centre of red section of bag, with the edges of tab about 3½ in. (8·9 cm) down from the top edge. Fix down with 3 eyelets in a row, following the instructions which come with the kit.

Repeat all above instructions for a red tab on the blue section on the same side of bag. Take the blue handle piece and spread the back with glue. Leave to set. Fold under ½ in (13 mm) down each side to meet in the centre, and press down well. Slip one end through gilt ring. Fold 1 in. (2·5 cm) back on to handle and glue down. Fix with 3 eyelets in a row, following maker's instructions. Repeat for other end of handle on the blue section of this side of bag.

Then repeat same methods for attaching red handle, tabs and rings on other side of bag.

18

Clown laundry bag (for nursery)

See page 21

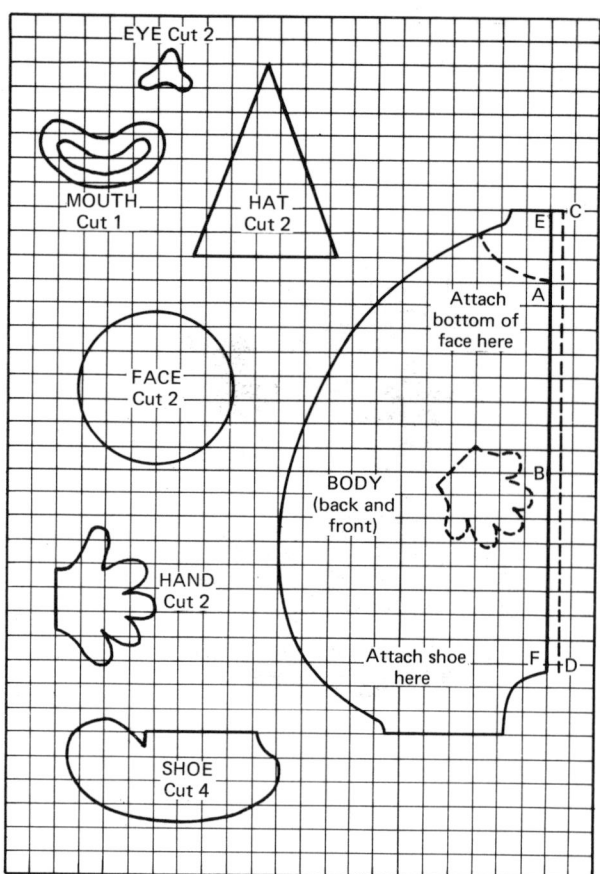

You will need

24 in. × 52 in. (62 cm × 132 cm) ticking (usually sold 59 in. wide)

7 in. × 14 in. (18 cm × 36 cm) white felt for face

8 in. × 12 in. (20 cm × 30 cm) green felt for hat and hands

13 in. × 18 in. (33 cm × 46 cm) cerise felt for mouth, boots and dots 2 in. × 4 in. (5 cm × 10 cm), turquoise felt for eyes and dots

1 in. × 1 in. (2·5 cm × 2·5 cm) red felt for nose

Oddments of assorted colours for 1 in. diameter dots

Approx $\frac{1}{4}$ oz (7 g) 4 ply wool for hair

Paper for pattern

Matching threads

Copydex

Brass ring 1 in. (2·5 cm) diameter

Pattern

Each square = 1 in. (2·5 cm).

Mark your paper up into 1 in. squares and copy your pattern on to it from the diagrams given. Cut out all pieces.

Making up

$\frac{1}{4}$ in. (6 mm) seams are allowed on ticking.

Cut out all parts required in felt and ticking. With right sides facing, stitch front pieces up together up centre seam, leaving gap open from A to B. Press seam open flat and hem down edges all round inside of gap.

Place back and front together with right sides facing. Tack and stitch all round every edge to form a bag. Turn to right side through front gap and press seams all round.

Using only a little *Copydex*, glue lower edge of one hat section on to one face section, and edge stitch along. Glue face features in place as shown in picture and edge stitch round each piece. Glue hat dots down centre front of hat and secure with a large cross stitch. Glue and tack bottom of completed face front on to front of ticking bag in position indicated on pattern.

Glue and stitch back hat and back face together as for front. Glue them to back of face and back of bag, carefully meeting and matching all edges. Stitch all round edges and through all thicknesses at bottom of face.

Make a bunch of wool loops about 2$\frac{1}{2}$ in. (6·3 cm) long and stitch to each side of head as shown in photograph.

Glue button dots in place as shown and secure each one with a large cross stitch. Glue hands in position indicated and stitch all round edge of each.

Place two shoe sections together and edge stitch all round on right side leaving top open. Fit over end of leg on ticking and stitch through all thicknesses to secure. Glue a button dot on shoe and secure with a large cross stitch. Repeat for other shoe.

Stitch brass hanging ring out of sight on to back of hat.

Puff out body with tissue paper before gift wrapping.

Fluffy hen tea cosy

See page 25

You will need

12 in. × 32 in. (30 cm × 80 cm) beige fur fabric for outer cover

12 in. × 32 in. (30 cm × 80 cm) red warm lining fabric

9 in. × 10 in. (23 cm × 25 cm) brown felt for head, tail and eyelids

pages 20 and 21
Victorian doll nightdress case
Clown laundry bag

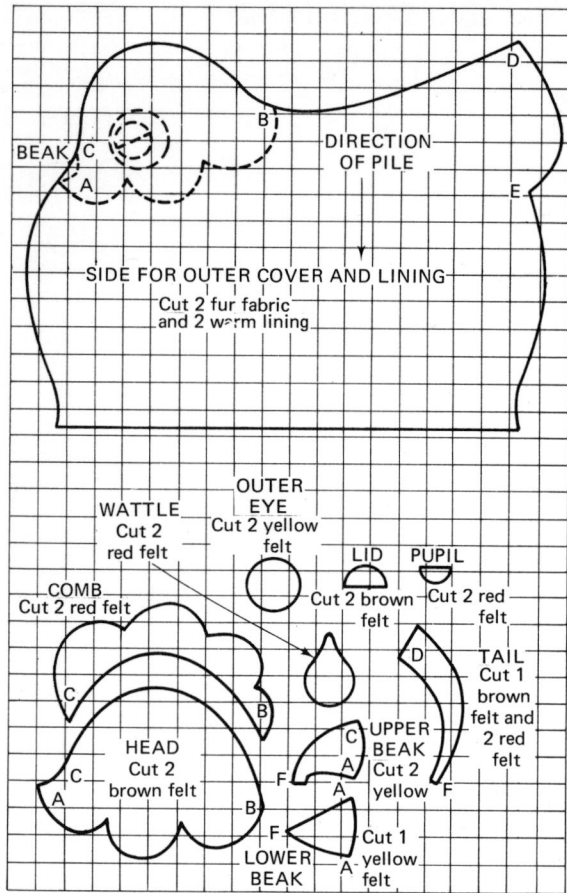

Pattern labels in diagram:

BEAK C / A
B / D
DIRECTION OF PILE
E
SIDE FOR OUTER COVER AND LINING
Cut 2 fur fabric and 2 warm lining

WATTLE
Cut 2 red felt

OUTER EYE
Cut 2 yellow felt

LID
Cut 2 brown felt

PUPIL
Cut 2 red felt

COMB
Cut 2 red felt

TAIL
Cut 1 brown felt and 2 red felt

HEAD
Cut 2 brown felt

UPPER BEAK
Cut 2 yellow

LOWER BEAK
Cut 1 yellow felt

Seam allowances

$\frac{1}{4}$ in. (6 mm) allowed all round body and body lining

$\frac{1}{2}$ in. (13 mm) allowed round bottom edge

Felt is edge-stitched on right side $\frac{1}{8}$ in. (3 mm) from edge except where otherwise stated

To make

Mark your paper up into 1 in. (2·5 cm) squares and copy the patterns on to it from the diagrams given.

Cut out all pattern pieces, then cut out all parts required in fur fabric, lining and felt. Remember that the fur pile should run downwards.

Place both sides of outer cover together with right sides facing. Tack and stitch all round, leaving bottom edge open. Join the two lining pieces together in the same way. Clip round curves and corners, and turn outer cover to right side. Clip round curves and corners of lining and ease up inside outer cover, so that the wrong sides of each are facing. Trim off about $\frac{1}{8}$ in. (3 mm) all round bottom of lining. Turn under $\frac{1}{2}$ in. (13 mm) hem all round the bottom and stitch neatly, so that the stitches go through the lining and just catch the back of the fur fabric.

Head First take the 2 comb pieces and stitch together all round the scalloped edges. Sandwich this 'double' comb between the top of both head sections, matching CC and BB. Stitch all round top of head from A to C to B. Slip the felt head and comb over the fur fabric head, still matching the lettering. Tack in place, then oversew all round the scallop edges. Push the head lining well up while you work, and pass oversewing stitches right through the lining to keep it in place inside the cosy.

6 in. × 9 in. (15 cm × 23 cm) red felt for comb, wattles, pupils and tail

4 in. × 4 in. (10 cm × 10 cm) yellow felt for eyes and beak

Matching threads

Paper for pattern (or buy graph paper)

Approx $\frac{1}{2}$ oz (14 g) kapok for filling beak cottonwool would do)

22

Eyes Place one outer eye in position shown and oversew all round. Stitch pupil and eyelid on to outer eye. Repeat for other eye.

Beak Tack and stitch both upper beak sections together from F to C. Stitch in lower beak matching AA, FF, and AA. Fill beak softly and pin to front of head, matching all lettering. Slip stitch all round, curving the sides of the beak slightly outwards.

Wattle Stitch the point of one wattle piece in the centre of chest, immediately under the beak, with the round part pointing slightly outwards. Stitch in place with a firm cross stitch. Stitch the point of other wattle on to the first, taking the threads right through to the lining.

Tail Place the brown tail piece between two red tail pieces, and tack together from D to E. Pin in place on cosy, matching DD and EE. Part the pile of the fabric and stitch tail to the actual seam line, again taking stitches through to the lining. Pull stitches firmly to 'sink' them in the pile.

Now work over all the fur fabric seams with the eye end of a needle, picking out any pile which is caught in the seams. Give a final brush to fluff up the pile.

NB This tea cosy, being partly made from felt, would have to be dry cleaned. Goddard's *Dry Clean* in spray form is good for cleaning felt.

Brocade work bag

See page 68

You will need

1 pair bag handles (those shown are 9 in. (23 cm) wide across the bar)

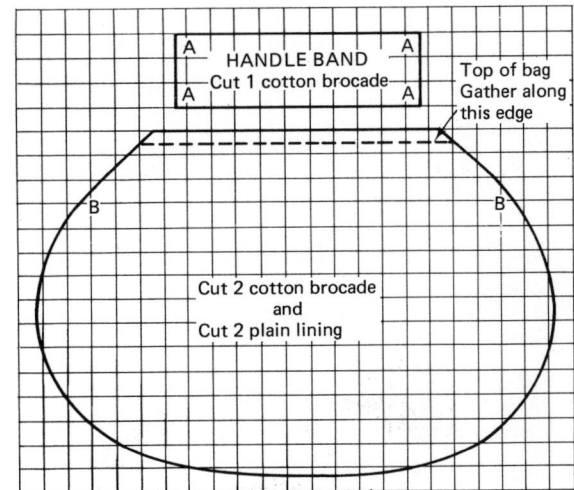

½ yd (46 cm) printed furnishing cotton brocade 48 in. wide
½ yd (46 cm) plain lining 48 in. wide
1¼ yd (122 cm) approx ruching fringe
Matching threads
Paper for patterns or graph paper

To make

Seams
½ in. (13 mm) allowed all round outer cover
⅝ in. (16 mm) allowed all round lining

Mark your paper up into 1 in (2·5 cm) squares, copy the pattern on to it from the diagrams given (or use graph paper), and cut out. Then

pages 24 and 25

23

cut out all pieces required in fabrics. Tack the ruching all round the sides and bottom of one outer cover section from B to B, on the right side of fabric, with the fringes pointing inwards, towards centre of section.

Place the other side of outer cover on to the first, right sides facing, with the ruching sandwiched between, and stitch all round from B to B. Turn to right side, place the two lining pieces together, right sides facing, and stitch all round from B to B. Clip round curves. Slip lining inside cover, so that wrong sides of cover and lining are facing.

Tack lining and cover together up and down each side gap from A to B. Then make hem all round each gap, turning cover and lining together over and over again to the inside. Oversew neatly to lining. Reinforce bottom of each gap with a few extra stitches.

Fold at least $\frac{1}{2}$ in. (13 mm) of each short end of handle band under to wrong side, and catch stitch along. The amount you fold under will depend on the width of your handles — narrower handles will require the turning of more than $\frac{1}{2}$ in. (13 mm) under, but this is a simple adjustment.

Run a gathering thread along top edge of one side of bag, through cover and lining. Draw up to fit one long side of handle band and fasten off. Tack one long side of handle band on to top edge of bag, over the gathers, with right sides of cover facing and matching the lettering. Stitch along this edge. Fold remaining long side of handle band over the cane handle bar, and tack down to stitching line on inside of bag. Stitch along. Oversew ends neatly and securely, but allowing the handles to move about freely. Repeat for attachment of handle to other side of bag.

Covered coathangers

See page 28

RUCHED PRINT COVER
You will need

Wooden coat hanger
2 in. × 36 in. (5 cm × 92 cm) sheet wadding
Approx 12 in. (30 cm) length ribbon, $\frac{1}{2}$ in. (13 mm) wide
$4\frac{3}{4}$ in. × 36 in. (12 cm × 92 cm) piece of printed cotton
Scrap of ribbon for bow
Matching threads

To make

Pad hanger by winding strips of wadding round and round, and stitching securely at each end. To bind the hook, fold 1 in. (2·5 cm) of one end of ribbon over top end of hook. Hold firmly down and bind remaining ribbon over this end and very tightly all down the hook. Stitch end to wadding at base of hook.

Fold piece of printed cotton in half lengthwise, with right sides facing. Stitch across both short ends. Turn to right side. Fold long raw edges under about $\frac{1}{4}$ in. (6 mm) to inside, press these turnings and a crease line along folded edge. Slip padded hanger inside the 'bag', so that the seam runs along the top of the hanger. Pin ends of cover to padding at ends of hanger to keep in place while working.

Join seam edges with small running stitches, working neatly round the hook. Then work small running stitches along the bottom crease, and pull both ends of thread to form straight and even gathers all along. Make a bow from ribbon scrap and sew to hanger at base of hook.

VELVET COVER
You will need

Wooden hanger
2 in. × 36 in. (5 cm × 92 cm) sheet wadding
Approx 18 in. (46 cm) length pink velvet ribbon
   ½ in. (13 mm) wide
1 yd (92 cm) navy velvet ribbon 1½ in. (3·8 cm)
   wide
½ yd (46 cm) lace edging
Matching threads

To make

Pad the hanger as for the ruched hanger. Measure the length of the hook and cut twice this length from narrow pink ribbon. Fold this ribbon in half and oversew edges together to form a tube. Slip over the hook and stitch end to wadding at base of hook.

Fold wide velvet ribbon in half and turn in raw ends to fit length of hanger. Oversew two long edges together and slip hanger inside so that the open edges are at the top. Slip the hanger inside the 'bag' and oversew top edges together, working neatly round the base of hook.

Run a gathering thread along inner edge of lace, draw up and stitch round all edges of remaining length of pink velvet ribbon (approx 1¼ in.) — 32 mm.

Stitch finished rosette to hanger at base of hook.

FELT 'CLOWN' COVER
You will need

Small wooden hanger (approx 10½ in. (27 cm)
   long)
3 in. × 12 in. (7·6 cm × 30 cm) blue felt
3 in. × 5 in. (7·6 cm × 13 cm) white felt for face
Scraps of turquoise, pink and red felts for
   features

Scraps of yellow wool for hair
Small ball of cotton wool
Copydex
Matching threads
Paper for hanger pattern

To make

From blue felt, cut a strip ¼ in. × 12 in. (6 mm × 30 cm). Spread a thin layer of *Copydex* for about ½ in. (13 mm) along one end, and fold over end of hook. Wind remaining strip of felt round and round hook, glueing at base of hook to secure'

Place hanger on paper and draw all round it. Draw a second line all round, ¼ in. (6 mm) further out from the first, to allow for turnings. Cut out pattern, and mark round this twice on to blue felt. Cut out both pieces. Place one on each side of hanger and oversew edges together all round, with small neat stitches.

To make head, cut out two circles of white felt, each 2 in. (5 cm) diameter. Place them together with a knob of cotton wool sandwiched in between, and oversew all round edges.

Cut a ⅝ in. (16 mm) diam. nose circle from pink felt and glue to face, just below centre. Cut a mouth crescent approx 2¼ in. (5·7 cm) wide from red felt, and glue to face under nose.

pages 28 and 29
Covered coathangers
Circular guest or make-up towel; towelling bath mitt;
back scrubber

27

Cut 2 triangles from turquoise felt about $\frac{5}{8}$ in. (16 mm) high and $\frac{1}{2}$ in. (13 mm) wide for eyes, and glue to face. When glue has set, stitch round each piece.

Cut wool into lengths of about 1$\frac{1}{2}$ in. (3·8 cm) and glue several strands to the back of each side of the face, and a few more to top of head. When glue has dried, unravel strands to make hair fluff out, and trim if necessary.

Spread a little glue across top of face at the back, and press against hanger for a second or two. When glue has dried, stitch face to hanger where they are glued together at the back for extra security.

WOOL WOUND ROUND WIRE
You will need

Wire coat hanger
Approx $\frac{1}{2}$ oz (14 g) thick wool in each of two colours (red and yellow)

To make

Straighten hanger into shape if necessary. Start the winding at the base of the hook, and use two colours at once, keeping them flat and untwisted. Continue round, winding tightly, and with the strands pushed close together, until frame is covered. Bind the hook with plain red.

Lay end of wool about 1 in. (13 mm) along end of hook and bind rest of wool over this, and then close together all round the hook to base. Secure end with a dab of glue.

For the tassel, cut about 5 red and 5 yellow strands of wool, each 7 in. (18 cm) long. Fold them over top of hanger (5 each side of hook). Hold the bunch together and wind red wool tightly round it as close to the top as possible. Using a darning needle, thread end of wool down through binding into the bunch. Unravel ends of wool to make a fluffy tassel.

Circular guest or make-up towel

See page 29

You will need

Circle of towelling 20 in. (50 cm) diameter
Approx 2 yd (184 cm) white fringing or other pretty edging
Brass curtain ring
Scrap of white *Orlon* or *Courtelle* knitting yarn
Matching threads

To make

It is simple to make a large 'compass'. Cut a strip of card or stiff paper 11 in. long and about $\frac{1}{2}$ in. (13 mm) wide. Push a drawing pin (thumb tack) through one end. Mark a point 10 in. (25 cm) from centre of drawing pin and make a hole. Press drawing pin, with card, through the towelling, and the point of a pencil through the hole at the other end of the card. Now mark the edge of towel by drawing the pencil right round in a circle, keeping fabric flat and card taut, cut out round pencil line.

Make a narrow hem all round edge of towel and stitch on edging.

Cover the brass ring by working buttonhole stitch all round it in white yarn. Stitch to centre of towel circle.

Printed cotton lampshade

See page 41

You will need

White plastic-coated collared frame with a table light fitting. Bottom diameter 12 in. (30 cm)

14 in. × 42 in. (35 cm × 107 cm) printed cotton
  for cover
14 in. × 42 in. (35 cm × 107 cm) white cotton
  for lining
3½ yd (3·2 m) white fringe 1 in. (2·5 cm) wide
1½ yd (1·3 m) bobble fringe
Approx 12 in (30 cm) braid
Matching threads
Approx 1 yd (92 cm) elastic
½ yd (46 cm) white tape 1¼ in. (32 cm) wide

To make

Cut covering and lining fabrics to make straight
strips, each 13½ in. × 40 in. (35 cm × 1·1 m).
Place lining fabric on to cover fabric, with wrong
sides facing. Tack together and continue to
work throughout as if they were one thickness
of fabric.

Fold the fabric strip in half lengthwise, with
right sides of cover fabric facing. Pin short ends
together for side seam.

Check the measurement of the circumference
of the bottom ring on frame. Adjust pins at side
seam, if necessary, to fit closely. Stitch side
seam and press. Turn the upper edge of the
fabric 'tube' over ¼ in. (6 mm) and then over
again, to make a ½ in. (13 mm) hem. Stitch hem
all round, but leave a 1 in. (2·5 cm) opening for
threading the elastic. Turn and stitch lower edge
of tube as for upper edge. Turn tube right side
out. Apply fringes to lower edge. Stitch white
fringe all round, 1 in. (2·5 cm) from bottom edge
and with the fringe facing downwards. Stitch
the bobble fringe above the white fringe all
round, so that the lower edge of the bobbles
just meets against the top edge of the white.
Stitch another length of white fringe all round
above the bobbles, but to face upwards. (To
finish ends of braids and fringes, turn each under
¼ in. (6 mm) and stitch down neatly).

Thread elastic through bottom hem, and
leave ends hanging loose. Thread elastic
through top hem, and leave hanging loose.
Place cover on to frame. Draw up top and
bottom elastic until the cover fits tightly over
the frame, so that the lower hem is drawn towards
the centre, inside the bottom ring. The upper
hem will be drawn towards the centre at the
top. Fasten off the ends of the elastics securely.
Adjust the top 'draw-in' to make it even all the
way round. Adjust the gathers evenly all round.

Make collar fringes. These have to be
mounted on to the white tape to make them
detachable. Arrange the fringes in exactly the
same order as for those round the bottom, and
stitch them along the tape so that the tape will
not show at front. Make these detachable
fringes 16 in. (42 cm) long. Turn under ½ in.
(13 mm) at each end, and stitch down neatly.

Fit fringes round neck of frame and pull close
in tightly. Catch stitch ends together to hold
firmly in position. Hooks and eyes can be used,
but they are more bulky.

Stitch braid round the edge of the opening
on the top of the shade, so that the hem stitches
are covered.

To remove cover for washing

Undo stitches joining ends of collar fringes, and
remove from shade. Turn the shade upside
down. Carefully ease the elasticated hem over the

pages 32 and 33
Dried flower arrangement
Pressed flower picture

bottom ring all round. Turn shade right way up and slip cover upwards and off the frame.

Reverse these procedures for replacing on the frame.

Towelling bath mitt

See page 29

You will need

Materials

Printed towelling
Plain towelling
Bias binding
Matching threads
Graph paper for pattern

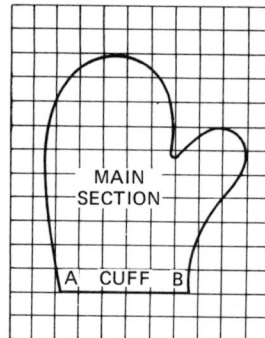

To make

Copy the pattern on to the graph paper from the diagram given and cut out. Mark and cut out both hand pieces, first in printed towelling and then in plain towelling, reversing the pattern for the second printed piece. Arrange pieces for sewing. Lay one printed section right side facing downwards, then one pair of plain sections on this, followed by the second printed piece with right side facing upwards. Carefully match pieces together all round thumb and bottom edges etc. Tack all round through all four thicknesses, leaving bottom open. Then tack round bottom through two layers only. Stitch bias binding all round mitt, then round opening, leaving enough binding at the end to make a small loop for hanging. Fold bias over on to other side of mitt and stitch all round. Fold and stitch bias to make the loop. With careful working, the bias may be applied in one piece all round, but be sure to leave enough to make the loop. Press binding flat all round.

Back scrubber

See page 29

You will need

10 in. × 20 in. (25 cm × 50 cm) printed towelling
1½ yd (1·3 m) thick cotton cord or piping cord
1 card bias binding
9 in. × 19 in. (22·8 cm × 48·2 cm) *Terylene* wadding
Matching threads

To make

Cut towelling to size 9 in. × 19 in. (23 cm × 48 cm), making sure that edges are straight and corners square. Fold towelling in half lengthwise, with wrong sides facing.

Cut wadding to size 8 in. × 18 in. (20 cm × 46 cm), and fold in half lengthwise. Place folded wadding inside folded towelling and tack seam round the three raw edges.

Tack and stitch bias binding to both the long edges.

Cut the cord in half. Bind or stitch the ends of one piece together. Lay the joined part on one end of towelling pad. Fold about 1 in. (2·5 cm) of towelling over through rope ring, then stitch down neatly, covering rope join.

Repeat for loop at other end.

Fur pile shoe polisher

See page 24

You will need

8½ in. × 13 in. (22 cm × 33 cm) fur fabric
2 wooden curtain rings approx 1½ in. (3·8 cm) diameter
Matching threads

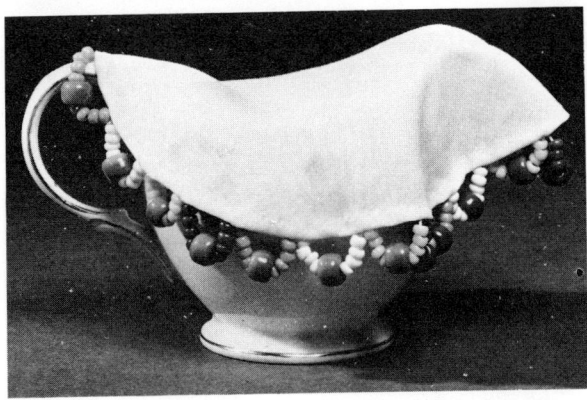

2 pieces ribbon, each 3 in. × 1 in. (7·6 cm × 2·5 cm) wide

To make

Fold fur fabric in half lengthways, with right sides facing. Stitch together along long sides and one short end. Turn to right side, fold under turning at open end, and stitch along. Using double thread, gather along edge of one end and pull up tightly. Fasten off. Repeat for other end of polisher. Pass one piece of ribbon through one ring. Fold ends of ribbon under, stitch firmly together and on to the polisher at the same time. Repeat for ring at other end of shoe polisher.

Beaded jug cover

The material used for jug covers should be fine enough to keep out insects, etc, and woven loosely enough to let the air in. Soft fine net, muslin, organdie and cotton lawn are all suitable. If you do not feel like sewing a tiny hem all round the edge, a simple ladies' handkerchief makes a good substitute, and is quicker.

Jug covers may be round or square; draw round a saucer or plate to mark a circle.

If you have no beads, old necklaces are found readily in Oxfam shops, and many junk shops, but wash them before use. Plastic beads are too light for the purpose, so keep to glass, china or wooden beads.

Threading the beads is very simple, and great fun. Plan a design before starting.

To make

Cut your material to the size required, and sew a neat, narrow hem all round the edge. Measure round the edge of the jug cover and mark faintly, with a pencil dot, into evenly-spaced divisions approximately 1 in. (2·5 cm) to 1½ in. (3·8 cm) apart. Attach thread at one of the pencil dots, thread on required beads in their order, and then take needle on through edge of cover at next pencil dot. Make an extra stitch or two to secure. Thread more beads, work on to next pencil dot and secure. Continue all round in this manner until beading is completed. Iron out any creases in the jug cover.

Knitted golf club cover

See page 24

You will need

Scraps of Courtelle, double crepe or double knitting wool in navy
Scraps of red, blue and pink felt
Matching threads and darning needle
Milwards knitting needles disc 8
Copydex

pages 36 and 37
Tissue box cover; lavender sachets
Pot pourri; pomander; lavender sachet

To make

With red wool cast on 40 stitches
Rib: K2, P2, for 1¼ in. (3·2 cm)
Change to white wool
Rib: K2, P2, for ¾ in. (19 mm)
Change to navy wool
Rib: K2, P2, for 3¼ in. (8·3 cm)
Change to white wool
Stocking st. for 3 in. (7·6 cm)
Change to navy wool
Knit 2 rows plain, then ¼ in. (6 mm) stocking
    stitch
Change to red wool and knit 2½ in. (6·4 cm) in
    garter stitch
    Break off wool about 12 in (30 cm) from
end of last row of work. Thread end through
needle and pass through each stitch in turn on
knitting needle. Draw wool right through and
pull up taut. Fasten off securely. Stitch sides
together, taking care to match the stripes.
When making the face, make sure that the seam
comes down the centre back. Make a pompom
from remainder of navy wool and stitch to top
of head.

For eyes, cut out 2 circles of blue felt, each
1 in. (2·5 cm) diameter. Cut a V section out of
each one.

For nose, cut out a crescent of red felt. Draw
round a small glass to get the lower curve,
then move the glass up a little to get the upper
inside curve.

Spread a little *Copydex* on the back of each
section and glue in position. Stitch neatly round
each.

Frog bean bag

See page 17

You will need

9 in. × 14 in. (23 cm × 36 cm) plain coloured
    velvet (or other firm fabrics)
9 in. × 14 in. (23 cm × 36 cm) printed needle-
    cord (or other firm fabrics)
11–12 oz (312–340 g) lentils or rice for filling
3 in. × 4 in. (7·6 cm × 10 cm) toning felt for feet
3 in. × 4 in. (7·6 cm × 10 cm) contrasting felt
for eyes and feet
2 shiny black beads for pupils
Matching threads
Paper for pattern
Scale   1 square = 1 in. (2·5 cm)

To make

(¼ in. (6 mm) seam allowance)

Copy the patterns on to the graph paper from
the diagrams given, and cut out each piece.
Place pattern pieces on felt and fabrics, mark
round each, and cut out all pieces as directed
on patterns.

Fold the underbody in half lengthways, with
right sides facing, and stitch dart from C to D.
Tack upper body and underbody together with
right sides facing. Leaving gap for turning and
filling from A to B, stitch all round frog. Work
a second row of stitching for extra strength
round the seams. Clip carefully at curves and
corners of seam allowances. Turn to right side
and ease out all seams with a wooden spoon
handle to ensure a well-shaped toy.

Pour in the lentils or rice and stitch across
gap very neatly, using ladder stitch. Stitch one
eye circle to each side of head at A and B.
Stitch a black bead to one circle, then pass
needle and thread through head to stitch
second bead to other eye circle, at the same time

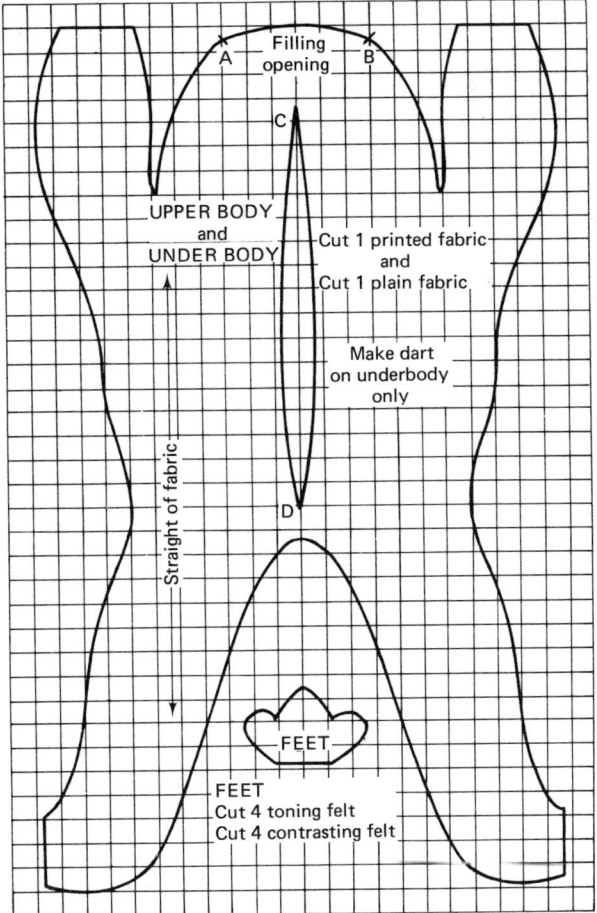

Filling opening

A B

C

UPPER BODY
and
UNDER BODY

Cut 1 printed fabric
and
Cut 1 plain fabric

Make dart
on underbody
only

Straight of fabric

D

FEET

FEET
Cut 4 toning felt
Cut 4 contrasting felt

Miniature hobby donkey

See page 73

You will need

Approx 10 in. (25 cm) length of dowelling $\frac{3}{8}$ in. (9 mm) diameter
5½ in. × 9 in. (14 cm × 23 cm) green felt for head
5 in. × 7 in. (13 cm × 18 cm) pink felt for mane and nostrils
Turquoise felt for ears, 4 in. × 5 in. (10 cm × 13 cm)
Scraps of black, white and yellow felts for eyes, harness and buckles
Kapok
Copydex
Card for pattern
A small bell (optional, and may be found in most craft shops)

To make

Mark the card into 1 in. (2·5 cm) squares and copy the pattern on to it from the diagrams given. Cut out. Cut out all pieces in felt as indicated in the pattern. Place the mane in position round the edge of the head, matching AA and BB on wrong side. Lay the other side of head on this, matching carefully all round. Sew all round, through all thicknesses leaving bottom of neck open. Fill nose and face firmly with *kapok*. Wind some *kapok* round one end of dowel rod and insert into head. Stuff the rest of the head and neck, at the same time surrounding the stick firmly with *kapok* so that it

pulling the thread slightly to form 'eye sockets'.
Now make the feet. Stitch together one piece of each colour by stab stitching all round 'toes'. Then oversew the straight edge of felt to straight edge of one leg. Repeat for other three feet. Work the filling in and out of each leg to get it running freely inside the toy.

pages 40 and 41
Shell picture
Printed cotton lampshade; suede owl

39

does not wobble about. Leave about $\frac{1}{2}$ in. (13 mm) round the bottom edge free from *kapok.* Spread glue all round inside of felt and draw in firmly against dowel rod. Bind round tightly with thread before glue dries out. Finish neatly by gluing a strip of felt all round the join.

Eyes Glue pupils on to eye whites, then stick complete eye in position as shown.

Ears Fold each ear in half, with a dab of glue in the fold at the bottom. When the glue is set, spread a little glue on lower edge of one side of folded ear, and press in position on the head.

Harness Cut black felt in $\frac{1}{8}$ in. (3 mm) wide strips and glue to face as shown in photograph. Cut 2 tiny circles of yellow felt and stick in position where the straps meet. Glue nostrils in position on nose.

Mane Cut the felt mane into $\frac{1}{8}$ in. (3 mm) wide strips all along, from outside edge to the seam line of the neck. Ruffle the strands after cutting.

Stitch bell, if used, firmly to base of neck at the front. Round off the end of the rod with sandpaper and make sure it is very smooth.

Tissue box cover *See page 36*

You will need

$\frac{1}{4}$ yd (23 cm) printed cotton 36 in. (92 cm) wide
$2\frac{1}{2}$ yd (230 cm) decorative braids
Copydex
Matching threads
Note $\frac{1}{4}$ in. seams are allowed all round

To make

Cut 2 pieces fabric $3\frac{1}{4}$ in. × $10\frac{1}{2}$ in. (8·3 cm × 27 cm) for sides
Cut 2 pieces fabric $3\frac{1}{4}$ in. × $5\frac{1}{4}$ in. (8·3 cm × 13 cm) for ends
Cut 1 piece fabric $5\frac{1}{4}$ in. × $10\frac{1}{2}$ in. (13 cm ×

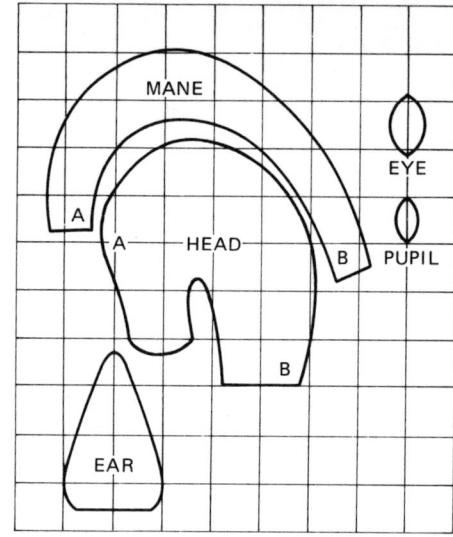

27 cm) for top

With right sides facing, join the four short ends of side pieces to form an oblong. With right sides facing, stitch this oblong all round the top piece, matching the side seams to each corner carefully. Turn cover right side out. Tack $\frac{1}{4}$ in. (6 mm) over on to right side all round the bottom edge. Stitch or glue the braid on all round, covering raw edges of the turnings.

Remove the opening tab on the tissue box, carefully pressing round the dotted line to obtain a clean edge. Slip the cover on the box and ease neatly into place. Gently run a pencil round the edge of the opening (it is easily felt) and cut this section. Glue or stitch braid round the opening, easing it evenly round curves and corners. Now glue or stitch braid over seams round top of box. It is easier to stick the braid on while the cover is on the box, as it provides a firm base for working.

Finally, oversew raw edges of seams inside for neatness, press all seams, and refit to box.

WORKING WITH DRIED AND PRESSED FLOWERS

Introduction

Drying and pressing flowers is a simple and most inexpensive craft.

There are several points to remember in connection with dried and pressed flowers. Never display any of the finished articles in sunlight, or the colours will fade. All material, whether it is being dried or pressed, must be stored in warm and airy places; a damp atmosphere will quickly turn the material limp and mildewy. Continue collecting throughout the year, there is always something worth drying and pressing at all seasons. Do experiment with different kinds and varieties of plants, especially wild flowers and plants. You can also buy the special seed, and grow your own everlasting flowers, and very colourful they are.

Drying flowers

The hanging method is the simplest and most commonly used method. It is suitable for most plants. Decide on a suitable drying space, such as an attic, loft or shed. Put up several string 'clothes lines'.

Gather flowers during very dry weather, just before they are in full bloom. Remove all leaves from flower stems. Tie flowers into small bunches, and hang upside down from the 'clothes lines'. Large flowers are best hung singly. Leave to dry out for a few weeks — the time varies according to the type of plant. When dry, the flowers are brittle and should be handled as little as possible to prevent them crumbling.

Dried flowers are suitable for a great variety of floral arrangements, collages, hangings, table centres, and even Christmas decorations. Some seed heads dry satisfactorily and look most attractive.

After drying, most flowers and seed heads are more delicate in colour, and appear rather subdued. They can be dyed simply and effectively. Hold the dried material heads down in a strong solution of dye, until desired depth of colour is reached. Remove and allow excess liquid to run out. Then stand the flowers upright in jars to dry out thoroughly. *Dylon* multi-purpose dye will do this job well.

Some suitable flowers for drying

Acanthus, Achillea, Alchemilla, Anaphalis, Catananche, Delphinium, Echinops, Larkspur, Golden Rod, Spirea, Statice, Physalis (Chinese Lanterns).

pages 44 and 45

Pebble-studded doorstop; painted stones; wooden stick raft; pebble pendant; pebble embedded in plastic; ornamental shell
Leather dice paperweight; shell and pebble owl; shells and pebbles embedded in resin; shell covered box; shell covered bangles

Some suitable seed heads for drying

Clematis and Old Man's Beard (best cut in bud to prevent falling), Honesty pods (when dry) peel off outer 'covers' to expose the lovely silver discs. Teasels (pick when green). Wild Parsley and other umbelliferous seed heads, and Poppy heads. Wheat and various grasses dry well if picked while still green.

Pressing flowers and leaves

The varieties of flowers and leaves suitable for pressing is infinite but remember that, after pressing, the colours are more delicate. White rose petals turn a lovely creamy colour, red geraniums remain quite bright after pressing, but some flowers turn to very attractive and unusual shades.

Collect plenty to allow for failures, and choose the best specimens. Gather leaves, ferns and stalks as well, as greenery is essential. Remember to pick dry, to avoid mildew forming.

All petals and leaves should be gently smoothed out on sheets of blotting paper, allowing a good amount of space between them. Thicker or fleshy flowers should be gently taken apart (they can be reassembled after pressing, at the design stage). Stems and ferns should be laid to their natural curve. Keep each variety of plant together, on its own sheet of blotting paper. Be very patient while you are doing this, and remember not to breathe too hard or the petals will blow off.

When all the flowers and petals are laid out, cover with a second sheet of blotting paper and place between the leaves of the 'pressing' book. Write the name(s) of the plants on slips of paper and stick to appropriate sheet, slightly projecting from the book, for easy identification.

Put the book or books in a dry, out-of-the-way place and weigh it down with something

heavy (bricks, large pebbles, old flat irons, etc). Don't open them again for *at least 6 weeks:* the petals will not have dried out properly and will be spoiled.

Equipment

Very little special equipment is necessary, but the following list will help:

Working with dried flowers

Strong string for hanging lines

Flat boxes or florist's boxes for storing dried material

Mounting card

Copydex

Oasis or *Styrofoam* shapes

Picture frames

Containers for arrangements

Sharp-pointed scissors, tweezers, cocktail sticks and other necessities as described in the instructions for individual articles

Large and heavy books such as old wallpaper sample books and telephone directories for pressing. Flower presses are available, but tend to be rather small.

Heavy weights to put on the books

Blotting paper

Mounting paper or stiff paper

Copydex

A knife with a rounded blade is most useful for lifting pressed flowers and sliding them in place

Other special items required will be found in the instructions

Storing preserved material

Dried flowers if you have room, may be left hanging on their original lines. They may also be stored in layers in long shallow boxes, with tissue paper between each layer.

Storage of pressed flowers is simple too, as

they can be left just where they are. It may be necessary to sort them out occasionally, discarding any failures. They may then be rearranged, but still left in heavy books, where they can be kept for years. Most important of all, store in a warm dry atmosphere.

Pressed flower picture

See page 33

You will need

Picture frame and glass, approx 16 in. × 13 in. (42 cm × 23 cm) (the frame and glass was found in a junk shop. The frame was stripped and well waxed and polished)
Coloured cardboard or photographic mounting board (cut to the same size as glass)
Copydex Sellotape X

Plants used

This list is given for guidance
14 white rose petals (they turn a creamy beige when pressed)
17 dark blue delphinium petals, pressed separately and arranged up a grass stem
30 dark blue clematis petals, pressed separately. The backs were used, as they turned a browny mauve. Also arranged up a grass stem
1 pale blue delphinium, pressed whole
6 grass seed heads and stems, pressed whole, with a curve
8 small wall ferns, pressed whole, with a curve

(the centres of the cream flowers are actually the clematis flower centres, pressed as for flowers and petals)

To make

Study the colour picture, and imagine a jar of water in the centre, from which the flowers are all curving outwards. Stick the large, creamy flowers in place first, then the stalks, and so on, on the coloured card until the picture is complete. Use only a smear of *Copydex* at the base of each petal, and just a very thin stroke of glue down stalks. The arrangement will also be kept in place by the glass.

Carefully place arrangement in your frame, tack frame backing in place, and seal edges with *Sellotape X*. The sealing is important because if damp gets in to the flowers, they will be ruined.

Pressed flower bookmark

You will need

Stiff drawing paper approx 1½ in. × 10 in. (3·8 cm × 25 cm) (or smaller if required)
Transparent *Fablon*
Pressed flowers (the design shown consists of one pink hydrangea, 2 blue hydrangeas, 4 violets, 2 dark red geranium buds, 4 honeysuckle flowers and 4 small leaves)
Copydex
Embroidery silk for end tassels

To make

Mark centre of drawing paper and stick centre flower in position. Continue working by simply sticking the pressed flowers as shown in the photograph, or making up your own simple design. Avoid thick overlapping of petals. When the completed design is stuck down, cover with transparent *Fablon*. Cut this a little larger all round than the paper with the flowers on it.

Peel away a very little of the backing paper and press edge of sticky transparent film firmly on to the design. Continue working down the bookmark, only peeling a little of the backing paper off at a time. Smooth film firmly and evenly over design to avoid air bubbles.

Trim off surplus *Fablon* all round the edges, and finish off by making tassels at each end.

Pebble plaque

Make several holes along top and bottom of marker about $\frac{1}{4}$ in. (6 mm) from edge. Cut a 4 in. (10 cm) to 5 in. (12 cm) length of embroidery silk and fold in half. Insert loop through one of the holes and pass loose ends through the loop. Pull gently to tighten the knot. Make the remaining tassels in the same way, but always pass each loop in the same direction through each hole.

Dried flower picture

You will need

An old frame (no glass is required)
Gold Spray paint for lacquer
A piece of felt for background, cut to the overall size of the frame
Small dried flowers in various sizes, colours and shapes
Copydex

To make

Discard the glass and take out the backboard. Clean the frame, and spray carefully and evenly with lacquer. Leave to dry. If the frame has an inner frame, spray both parts separately.

Cut the felt to the same size as the backboard. Spread *Copydex* over the back of the felt, and glue it on to the backboard, smoothing it over to avoid any wrinkles. Reassemble the frame, backboard, and inner frame (if used), so that the whole unit is complete. Fix the hanging fitting at this stage.

Work out a flower arrangement, and mark a little pencil dot right in the centre. Arrange the flowers on the felt as planned. If the picture in the photograph on page 50 is copied, make sure that the spaces between the flowers are all the same, and that the design is symmetrical.

Carry on in this way until design is complete. Blow very lightly over the picture to remove any odd bits.

Note Do not hang this picture in the sun or a very strong light in case of fading. Always hang in a dry place.

Dried flower collage

This collage is built up in an old frame which has been renovated. There is no glass, and the flowers are allowed to extent beyond the frame in an unusual and attractive manner.

The picture represents a bunch of flowers laid on a table. It was made up mainly from a ready-dyed-and-dried collection bought from the florist.

Work out a design and glue all the flowers in place, using a little *Copydex* only, overlapping and overlaying them to achieve a natural looking bouquet.

The collage should not be hung in sunlight, as the colours may fade. Keep in a warm, dry room: a damp atmosphere can turn dried or pressed flowers mildewy.

Pot pourri

The basic ingredient of good pot pourri is dried rose petals, especially the old-fashioned, sweet-scented, dark red varieties. However, for colour mixture and added scents, many other dried flower petals may be used.

You will need

Approx 6 oz (170 g) rose petals
Approx 1 oz (28 g) various other scented flower petals
1 level tablespoon of such spices as nutmeg, cinnamon, cloves, allspice

Measuring and marking with a pencil dot is worthwhile.

Now glue each flower head in place in turn. Start at the centre, using only tiny dabs of *Copydex* along the back of each head. Hold in place very gently for a couple of seconds for good adherence to the felt background. Finish the centre before starting the border pattern.

Mark the centre of top and bottom and each side and glue these 4 flowers down first. Then mark the centre between each one glued in place, and stick the next 4 flowers in position.

50

1 level tablespoon orris root or gum benzoin
Shallow, flat cardboard boxes or trays

To make

Collect the rose and flower petals on a very dry day — there must be no trace of moisture on any of the petals. Arrange them in the shallow boxes or trays, well spread out. Keep in a dark, warm place (the airing cupboard is ideal). Turn and move the petals about at least once a day. They must be allowed to dry out until very crisp, like cornflakes, and this will take 2 to 3 weeks.

When the petals are quite ready, put them in a large plastic bag. Add orris root or gum benzoin, together with the various chosen spices. Mix thoroughly by gently shaking the bag. Seal and store the bag for about three weeks, occasionally shaking it.

THE SACHET

See page 37

Cut out two circles of lace and two circles of fine muslin or organdie, all 5½ in. (14 cm) diameter. The muslin or organdie is for lining the lace to prevent small bits falling through. Stitch all four circles together on wrong side of work, leaving a 2 in. (5 cm) gap for turning. Turn to right side, fill with dried petal mixture, and stitch up gap. Then stitch wide frilly edging all round.

BOWL OF POT POURRI

Choose an attractive bowl, any size you wish, and fill with the pot pourri mixture. This is a delightful addition to any room, both in appearance and aroma. Turn the petals over occasionally to make sure they remain dry all through, and also to release more scent from below.

If you are making a gift of a bowl of pot pourri, it is essential that the top is sealed over tightly. Polythene, stretched over and secured with *Sellotape* or a rubber band, is ideal, and the contents can still be seen. This will seal in the scents as well as the contents. The recipient then simply removes the polythene when necessary.

Scented leaves   The following sweet-scented leaves may be used successfully in pot pourri mixtures:

Rosemary, thyme, lemon verbena, bay, mint, lavender, and other herbs.

They should be gathered and dried by the same methods as those used for petals.

Pomander

See page 37

You will need

1 medium-sized, thin skinned orange
3 oz (85 g) cloves
1 oz (28 g) orris powder (available from Boots Chemists)
1 oz (28 g) ground cinnamon
1¼ yd (122 cm) thin cord
¾ yd (2·7/3·66 m) white tape ¼ in. (6 mm) wide
6 in. (15 cm) scrap of ruched braid for trimming

To make

Tie half the tape tightly round the orange, thus dividing it into two sections. Tie remaining tape round orange at right angles to the first piece of tape. There are now four sections of bare orange skin. Cover these with cloves, pushing each clove right through the peel into the flesh. The cloves must be very close together, so that they touch each other.

Put the orris powder and cinnamon in a plastic bag. Shake well to mix. Place the clove-covered orange in this mixture and roll it about until the powder is well distributed over the pomander. Remove from bag and wrap loosely in greaseproof paper.

Store in a warm, dry place for 4 to 6 weeks, to dry right through (the airing cupboard is an ideal place, but not too near the hot tank). Remove greaseproof paper and tapes after storing and shake off excess powder.

Using the photograph as a guide, tie a double length of cord round pomander in the space left by tapes. Add a length of cord to make a hanging loop about 4 in. (10 cm) long.

The completed pomander must not be allowed to become damp, otherwise it will turn mildewy.

Lavender bags/sachets

See page 36

Sachets of various sizes and shapes are shown on pages 36 and 37. They are all made from small oddments of fabric, filled with dried lavender and finished with decorative edges, trimmings, coloured cord or velvet ribbon.

To prepare lavender

Cut the lavender on longish stems in very dry

weather and before the flower heads have opened fully. Lay the stems on trays or in flat, shallow boxes, with the heads all at the same end. Keep in a dark, warm place for 2 to 3 weeks until quite dry. When dry, gently run the fingers down each stem to rub off all the flower heads. Throw away the stems. Keep the dried lavender in an air-tight container until it is required for filling bags or sachets or adding to pot pourri mixtures.

Materials

Oddments of fine fabrics, lace, organdie, ribbons
Decorative edgings

To make

Cut the material into required shape — hearts and circles are attractive. Cut the organdie to the same size and shape. Place this on wrong side of covering fabric and continue to work as if they were a single thickness of material.

With right sides facing, stitch round bag, leaving an opening for turning and filling. Turn to right side and press seams. Fill with lavender and stitch across opening.

Bows, ribbons and other trimmings may now be added.

The *turquoise sachet* was gathered across (about two thirds of the way up from bottom) before tying fine cord tightly round.

The *pink heart* has a hanging loop, useful in a wardrobe. You could make tiny ones to hang on coathangers.

The *black and white sachet* is like a small cushion and would be attractive on a table in any room.

Dried flower arrangement

See page 32

The permanency of arrangements made up from dried flowers is most convenient for busy people, and for those who may not have access to fresh flowers. They are certainly an attractive form of winter decoration.

Dry the material as explained previously, or buy ready-dried flowers and grasses from flower shops.

Oasis is a valuable ingredient of a successful creation. It feels like hard sponge. It can be bought at flower shops in blocks of various shapes and sizes, and can be used many times before it disintegrates, and even then can be pressed wet into a container for fresh flowers.

The simple arrangement in the photograph on page 32 is based on a 3 in. (7·6 cm) diameter circle of *Oasis*. Plan the height and width required for the flowers, in good proportion to the container to be used. Place the *Oasis* into the container, to fit fairly snugly, and simply push the stalks into it. Start with the centre upright stalk to establish the height, and then insert a stalk at each side to establish the width. Continue by inserting remaining stalks at sides, with shorter ones to fill in across the front and centre of the arrangement. The finished work should look soft, and appear to flow. Avoid a stiff and rigid-looking arrangement.

WORKING WITH SHELLS AND PEBBLES

Introduction

Shellwork was a favourite pastime of the Victorians, and has returned as a fascinating and inexpensive hobby. Beautiful things can be made with shells or pebbles, or by combining the two. The materials needed do not cost very much, and little equipment is required. Shells are always pretty. Gathering them is good exercise, and working with them is a restful and satisfying pastime.

It is unlikely that identical shells and pebbles to those used for the items illustrated will be found. Nevertheless it is to be hoped that they will inspire the reader to make some beautiful things from her own collection.

Equipment

Generally speaking, for simple shell and pebble work little is needed in the way of tools:
Tweezers with pointed ends, for picking and positioning very small items
Wooden cocktail or orange sticks ⎱ for apply-
Small wooden or plastic spatulas ⎰ ing adhesive
A craft knife
A sheet of thick polythene to work on
A steady hand, and patience.

Adhesives

It is only necessary to apply adhesive to the area of the shell to be stuck down, so avoid using too much. Epoxy resin adhesives give the strongest and most permanent bond; several good brands are available, but select a quick-drying one. These adhesives come in a pack of two tubes, and you mix a little of each together. Mix only a small quantity at a time, otherwise it will dry up before it is finished.

For very light work, use transparent adhesive, such as *UHU*.

Tile cement works well with some shell and pebble work, but is slow to dry out.

Varnishing and colouring

The natural colouring of many shells is far too beautiful to be interfered with. However, much shell work is enhanced by finishing with a little varnish or colouring.

Here are some effective suggestions for preserving or improving colour:
(a)   Olive oil may be gently rubbed into the surface. This process may have to be repeated at intervals as it becomes absorbed, but avoid a greasy finish.
(b)   Varnish, if matt and not too shiny, is very satisfactory, but a shiny varnish gives a false appearance. Spray varnishes, polyurethanes and clear lacquers are available.
(c)   Nail varnish, especially the pale and pearly ones, can look superb, if used sparingly. Flowers in shell pictures can be beautifully tinted this way, but do experiment first. Try out on a dull

limpet shell, and you will see a transformation.
(d)   It is useful to know that tile cement and similar material may also be coloured quite simply. Use vegetable dyes (the cake icing ones) for small quantities, or a concentrated solution of a general purpose dye, such as *Dylon*, for larger quantities. In either case, stir well into ready-mixed tile cement, or stir well into water if using a type of cement you make up yourself.

Do remember that the amount of varnish or colouring you use depends on the amount of sheen and colour you require in your finished work. Start the process cautiously, you can always add another coat, but over-coloured or over-varnished work cannot be rectified.

Preparation of material

Stones and pebbles nearly always need cleaning up before use. Those found at the coast must be well scrubbed with scouring powder and rinsed to remove all traces of salt. Stones from inland just need a good wash. All stones may be rubbed gently with fine sandpaper to smooth them off if necessary, but it is best to avoid using very rough pebbles.

Shells need a different preparation. Often, the best specimens are still occupied by the 'animal'. In this case, boil them for 25 to 35 minutes, then pick out the meat with tweezers until the inside is completely clean. Rinse well. To remove any odour left in the shells, it is a good idea to soak them overnight in a strong solution of ordinary household bleach. Do make sure that all pebbles and shells are dry before using.

Storage of material

When thoroughly dry, store both shells and pebbles in little boxes. It is a good idea to segregate types and sizes, and label. Although they should not be affected by damp, it is best to store them in a dry atmosphere. Shell collections of course look wonderful simply displayed in open shelves or in glass fronted cupboards.

It should be pointed out, before you start on a project, that perfect symmetry is almost impossible to achieve. Perfect matching is rare, except with bivalves, that is, hinged shells like mussels, clams and so on.

Shell-covered boxes

See page 45

You will need

Boxes   wooden are the most suitable. Old cigar boxes and crystallised fruit boxes are ideal, and little boxes are available from craft shops for this type of work

Shells   all sorts of shapes and sizes, depending upon the shape and size of the box. You may prefer to use tiny shells in a small and pretty design, or a big and bold design with large shells

Adhesive   Epoxy resin adhesive is more suitable if the box is likely to be handled much

Spray varnish   } optional
Nail varnish colouring

Short length of dowelling, about $\frac{1}{2}$ in. (13 mm) thick, to cut into feet (centimetres), if required

Fine sandpaper

To make

It is important to plan the design to suit both the shells and the box, before sticking anything in place. Lay the shells in position on the top of the box, rearranging them until you are pleased with the effect; then and only then, start sticking them down. Shells round the sides of little boxes look best arranged in rows or simple border patterns. Over decoration tends to look more attractive than a meagre design or a thinly-covered box.

When the work is completed, a spray of varnish will bring out the colours and give a finish to any exposed areas of the box. Pearly nail varnish could be used to tint individual shells most attractively.

Do not forget to allow for the lid to open and shut easily. If it is hinged, it will be necessary to work carefully round the hinges.

If the box is large enough to need feet, cut the dowelling into equal lengths, $\frac{1}{4}$ in. to $\frac{3}{8}$ in. (6 mm to 9 mm). Stick into place at the corners. When glue has set, rub off rough edges of feet with fine sandpaper.

Shell-covered bangle

See page 45

You will need

An inexpensive plastic bangle
A variety of smallish shells
Epoxy resin glue
A small piece of fine sandpaper

To make

Sandpaper the bangle all round the outside area to be covered, to give a good surface for the glue to adhere to. Work out a design and arrangement of shells to make sure they will fit well and evenly round the bandle. Stick them all in place, following the instructions given with the glue. When all the shells have been applied, and the adhesive has set hard, paint a coat of polyurethane varnish all over each shell. This will enhance the colours. Leave to dry for 24 hours before wearing the bangle.

56

Ornamental shells

See pages 44 and 69

The two clam-like shells (see pages 44 and 69) were found on foreign shores. You may be lucky enough to find similar ones round the coasts of Britain, but most seaside gift shops sell them quite cheaply.

First scrub the shells in warm, soapy water and dry thoroughly before beautifying them. If the two halves are separated, stick them together with an epoxy resin adhesive. The marvellous colours of the smaller shell are brought out by painting over it with a coat of polyurethane matt varnish. The larger shell looks most exotic sprayed with gold lacquer.

Shells and pebbles embedded in plastic

See page 45

Small shells or pebbles embedded in clear plastic make exquisite paperweights. It is a simple way of transforming bits and pieces found on the beach into something beautiful, and the results are three dimensional. The process needs no skill whatever, and the work can be done anywhere in the house.

It is an extremely popular craft, and stamps, coins and flowers can be processed in the same way. All that is necessary is to measure some cold liquid plastic, add a hardener and pour into a chosen mould, working in shallow layers. The shells and pebbles are carefully laid on a set layer before more plastic is poured in.

More information, super ideas, and excellent instructions come with *Westbycast Embedding Kit.* See list of suppliers on page 95.

Shell picture

See page 40

A shell picture, or a collage, will never fail to arouse interest. They provide a wonderful way of using attractive material and, besides being very beautiful, are great fun to make.

Shells are an excellent medium for producing attractive flower pictures, which show off their delicacy to the best advantage. Abstract or symmetrical designs are most striking, but more effective as collages or shell plaques which do not require framing. They can be mounted on card or fabric, backed with a piece of plywood.

You will need

A picture frame (a new one, or a renovated one)
Black mounting card (or colour of your choice)
Adhesive
Pencil and ruler
Tweezers for placing smaller shells in position
An assortment of shells in various shapes, sizes and colours
Dried grass stalks, thin dry twigs, or dried flower stems — for stalks and stems

To make

Draw out a rough sketch of a flower arrangement. Then choose your shells and try them out in their places on the rough sketch. This will accustom you to the feel of the work, and will show you how simple it is to create flowers and flowery sprays.

Now draw very faint lines on the coloured card, copying the rough sketch and the arrangement you have decided to make.

Glue the flower container in place first. This could be something simple and informal, but some shells can be built up into wonderful formal and urn-like containers. Stalks and stems next, but at this stage, only glue the main ones in position.

Now, working from the centre upwards and outwards, stick the flowers, buds and 'leaves' where planned. When they are all securely placed, go over the work carefully and, where it appears necessary, stick in short lengths of stem and extra stalks. This is important as, otherwise, some of the flowers might look rather odd hanging, unsupported, in mid air!

Leave the work for all glue to set and dry thoroughly before framing. Discard the glass and fix the work in the frame very securely. Put a very firm backing to cover the back, as the work is heavy.

Pebble plaque

See page 48

You will need

A wooden picture frame or small wooden tray
Niclar Thikbed tile adhesive
Collection of small stones and pebbles
Black paint for edge of frame
Polyurethane clear matt varnish
Brushes
Plywood or hardboard for frame backing

To make

Remove glass, if any, from frame. Paint frame and leave to dry. Fasten plywood or hardboard to back very firmly with small panel pins. Spread tile adhesive all over inside of frame to fill entire area, keeping smooth and even, to a thickness of $\frac{1}{2}$ in. to 1 in. (13 mm to 2·5 cm).

Select your stones and make a rough drawing

of your planned design. Gently press the stones into the tile adhesive until they are half sunk. Continue until your arrangement is complete. Use a small knife or wood spatula to remove excess adhesive (there is plenty of time, as this brand does not dry out very quickly). Tidy up to ensure good straight edges to the adhesive. Leave to harden for about three days, and avoid moving.

When completely set, apply a coat of polyurethane varnish over the entire plaque, including the surround. Leave to dry before hanging.

Pebble pendant

See page 44

You will need

1 attractive pebble, approx $1\frac{1}{4}$ in. (3·2 cm) in diameter
$2\frac{1}{2}$ in. × 6 in. (6·3 cm × 15 cm) suede
UHU glue
15 in. to 16 in. (38 cm to 42 cm) length gold chain necklace (from Woolworths)
Approx 18 in. (46 cm) brass picture hanging wire
Polyurethane or other varnish

To make

From the piece of suede cut two circles, each about $2\frac{1}{4}$ in. (5·7 cm) diameter. Scrub the pebble well in warm soapy water, rinse, and dry out thoroughly. When dry, apply a coat of varnish to the better side of the pebble and also all round the edges. Leave to dry.

Spread a circle of glue on the right side of one piece of suede. Spread glue also over the back of the pebble (the unvarnished side). Leave both lots of glue to set for a few minutes, then press stone firmly down on to the suede.

Make a ring, slightly smaller than the pebble, of three strands from the brass hanging wire, twisting ends closely for a neat and secure finish. Thread a single strand of wire on to a strong needle. Holding the wire ring in place on the front of the pebble while you work, pass the needle from the back through to the front, over edge of ring, and through to the back again. Repeat three times more, at regular intervals. Twist ends of wire at back to secure firmly.

Spread a thin layer of glue all over back of suede holding the wired-down pebble, and another layer of glue all over wrong side of other circle of suede. Leave for a few minutes for glue to set, then press both pieces together very firmly, smoothing out air bubbles. Thread a short length of wire through both thicknesses of suede, then through a link of the chain and through to back of suede. Fasten ends by twisting wire securely, then glue a little patch of suede over ends of wire to prevent them catching in clothes.

Painted stones

See page 44

Stones for paperweights can be found in your own garden. Choose smooth ones of various shapes and sizes: small ones for paperweights, large ones for door stops.

Painting them is simple, and *Humbrol* enamels are available in tiny sizes.

You will need

Selection of smooth stones
Humbrol paints in bright colours
Several small brushes
White spirit or paint brush cleaner

To make

Wash and scrub stones well and leave to dry out thoroughly. Apply a coat of paint in your background colour to all visible surfaces of the stone. There is no need to paint the underside, but make sure it is smooth and won't scratch a good surface. Leave paint to dry and then add your own freehand designs or motifs. Clean brushes before using other colours.

It is wise to start at the centre of the design and work outwards. Remember that symmetrical or geometric designs are easier to work out. For ideas for designs or patterns, it is simply to adapt those found in children's books, and on various objects around the house.

Pebble-studded doorstop

See page 44

You will need

A large stone (about 2½ lb (1·13 kg) in weight)
A number of pretty small pebbles
Epoxy resin glue (it comes in a pack of two tubes)
Clear varnish

To make

Wash the large stone and all the little pebbles in warm, soapy water, rinse well, and leave to dry thoroughly. Examine the shape of the large stone, and work out a pattern or arrangement of the little stones in your mind. Mark it out on the stone, or draw roughly on paper.

Mix glue as instructed on the leaflet supplied. Apply glue to a small area on the large stone and also on the appropriate pebbles, then press the pebbles firmly in place. Work only small areas at a time, as this type of glue dries quickly.

Only mix a little glue at a time.

Stick the pebbles as close together as possible, continuing until design is complete and as much of the stone as you wish is attractively covered.

When all the glue has set hard, spray or paint a coat of clear varnish all over the work, and the uncovered areas of the large stone as well.

Shell and pebble animals

See pages 45 and 69

Making animals, birds and figures is great fun, and the results of assembling oddments in this way can be hilarious. You will find that the shapes of some stones are very suggestive of living creatures.

To assemble these novelties, use a fast-drying epoxy resin adhesive, so that the features do not slip about during the setting time.

When the glue has set hard, a spray of varnish is a simple and attractive way of finishing off.

The 'Owl' consists of a flattish stone for the body, 2 oval pebbles for the feet, and 2 smooth and well-worn limpets for the eyes. The nose is a piece of old fish bone, but a crab claw would be most effective.

The 'Mouse' consists of a whole mussel shell for the body, 2 tiny clam-shaped shells for ears, 2 tiny round shells for the eyes, and a small sea snail for the nose. (The body halves are separated and then glued firmly together.)

WORKING WITH LEATHER AND SUEDE

Introduction

Despite the many imitations of leather and suede which are available, we still prefer the natural material. Animal skins are sold by the square foot (square metre); they are easy to work, and may be found in most craft shops. There are also several firms which supply inexpensive offcuts of leather and suede, and these are well worth acquiring for making attractive small articles (see list of suppliers page 95). Offcuts are usually sold by the pound (kilogram).

Present-day leathers and suedes are obtainable in some superb colours and textures, and there are several excellent books to help you learn more about this interesting craft.

Materials

Lightweight leathers and suedes have been used for making the articles illustrated. Being soft and supple, they prove extremely versatile in design and workability.

Suede is the flesh side of the animal's skin. Textures can vary from a very silky finish to a rough but very attractive surface.

Sheepskin, goatskin and calfskin are all soft supple skins which are generally available and widely used.

Tools and equipment

A good sharp craft knife
A steel ruler to use as a straight edge for cutting
Hole puncher
Cutting-out scissors
Sharp-pointed scissors
Coloured or neutral leather polish, if required
Strong threads (button, linen or carpet)
Strong, sharp needles (for machining leather, a special needle is available)
Adhesives – different glues are used for different tasks (see individual instructions)

Marking and cutting leather and suede

Always mark round the pattern on the wrong side. Use a pencil, *never* a ball point pen which will smudge and leave unsightly marks on the leather. Keep an eye on the direction of the stretch, to ensure that it does not interfere with the outline of your pattern pieces.

Very soft or thin leathers can be cut with scissors, but proceed carefully. Cut as for felt and do not close the scissors or cut in short snips. Long, even cuts will prevent jagged edges. Straight lines in heavy leathers should be cut against a steel ruler with a sharp knife.

Holes for eyelets or decoration are very simply made with a hole puncher suitable for use in leatherwork.

Marking and stitching

Where possible, it is advisable to glue surfaces of leather together prior to stitching, to hold

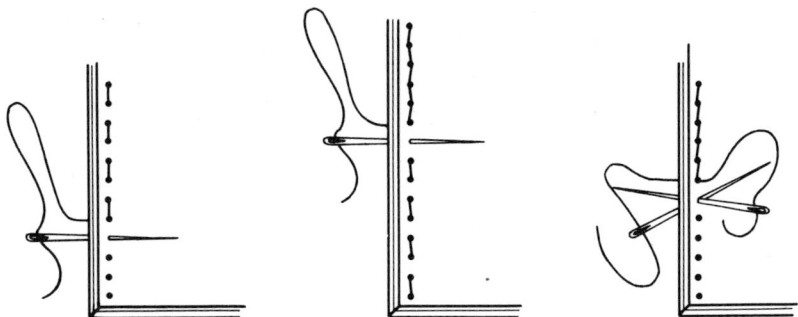

sections in position while working. Only a little glue is needed for this purpose. If two surfaces are to be joined by gluing alone, and not followed by stitching, then spread a layer of glue on each surface. Leave a minute or two for glue to set, and then press both surfaces firmly together. Stitching may be worked by machine, using strong thread and a leather machine needle on the lighter and softer leathers.

Heavier leathers and suedes may need to be stitched by hand. It is a great help, if possible, to run each section of leather separately through the unthreaded machine to make holes for easier hand stitching. If you do this, make sure that the holes will meet exactly opposite each other for perfectly even stitching. The stitches used in hand sewing are really very simple, and are explained in the diagrams.

Press studs and eyelets

Press studs and eyelets are now available in excellent small and inexpensive kits, including the necessary simple tools.

Leather dice paperweight

See pages 45 and 69

You will need

Approx 9 in. × 12 in. (23 cm × 30 cm) yellow leather
4 in. × 6 in. (10 cm × 15 cm) blue suede
Thread
Copydex
Lentils or rice for filling
Approx 4 in. × 4 in. (10 cm × 10 cm) cardboard for templates

To make

From the card, cut a 3 in. × 3 in. (7·6 cm × 7·6 cm) square template and a ¾ in. (19 mm) round template. Draw round these to mark the back of the leather. Cut out 6 squares in yellow 3 in. × 3 in. (7·6 cm × 7·6 cm) and 21 blue circles ¾ in. (19 mm) diameter.

Using templates, draw round each circle on to right side of leather squares to mark the position of the dots; use a little die as a guide, and space the dots symmetrically. Spread glue on back of each blue circle and over marked circle area on each yellow square. When glue is set, press each dot firmly into position and secure with a double stitch.

Glue and stitch edges of each square together

until a cube is formed, but leave about 1 in. (2·5 cm) open at one seam for filling. Using a funnel, pour in the filling until the die is just about full. Glue and stitch up gap.

Suede owl

See page 41

You will need

9 in. × 9 in. (29 cm × 29 cm) green suede for body and base
6 in. × 6 in. (15 cm × 15 cm) pink suede for eyes, wings and feet
$1\frac{1}{4}$ in. × 3 in. (3·2 cm × 7·6 cm) dark red suede for pupils
1 in. × $1\frac{1}{4}$ in. (2·5 cm × 3·2 cm) tan suede for beak
PAC or *UHU* glue
Matching strong thread
10–12 oz (283–340 g) rice or lentils for filling
9 in. × 9 in. (29 cm × 29 cm) card for pattern

To make

Mark the card into 1 in (2·5 cm) squares, copy the patterns on to it from the diagrams given and cut out the templates. Place templates on wrong side of suede and mark all round each piece with a pencil. Cut out all pieces required. *Stitching* All seams are joined by stitching edges together on the right side of work, $\frac{1}{8}$ in. (3 mm) from edge. They can be machined on soft suede, or otherwise by hand.

Take the body section and spread a $\frac{1}{8}$ in. (3 mm) wide line of glue all round the edges, except the bottom straight edge, on the wrong side. Leave for glue to dry.

Fold body piece to meet AA and BB, press edges together and stitch down this centre back

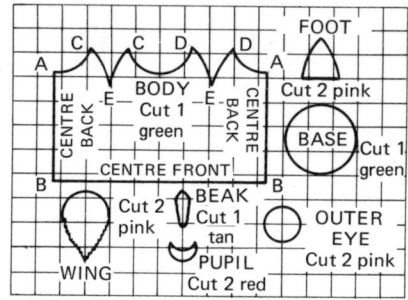

seam. Press edges of top of owl together matching CC and DD on ear points. Stitch from E to CC to DD to F. Pass all thread ends through to inside, and fasten securely.

Spread glue round edges of base and bottom of body, on wrong side. When glue has set, fit in base and press edges together as you ease it round. Stitch round, leaving a gap of approx $1\frac{1}{2}$ in. (3·8 cm) for filling.

Pour in filling through a funnel. Seal gap with glue and finish stitching.

Apply glue to both surfaces of each eye piece to be joined, leave to dry and stick in place on the face, as indicated on the pattern. Stick the beak to the face, so that the point hangs free to stick out a little.

Apply a little glue to wrong side of top of each wing only, and glue in place. Glue foot to base, so that curved part is just over the seam underneath.

Fringed suede pencil holder

See pages 65 and 73

You will need

Empty tin $4\frac{5}{8}$ in. high × 3 in. diameter (11·7 cm × 7·6 cm) make sure there are no sharp edges where top has been removed

A blue suede cut to size $3\frac{1}{2}$ in. × $9\frac{1}{2}$ in. (8·9 cm × 24 cm)

blue suede circle cut to $2\frac{3}{4}$ in. (7 cm) diameter

B yellow suede cut to size $2\frac{1}{2}$ in. × $9\frac{1}{2}$ in. (6·4 cm × 24 cm)

C green suede cut to size 2 in. × $9\frac{1}{2}$ in. (5 cm × 24 cm)

green *Felton* circle (*Fablon*) cut to $2\frac{3}{4}$ in. (7 cm) diameter for lining bottom

green *Felton* (*Fablon*) cut to size $4\frac{5}{8}$ in. × $9\frac{1}{2}$ in. (11.7 cm × 24 cm) for lining sides

PAC glue or *UHU*

To make

Study the diagrams and make sure that all the suede pieces are accurately measured and cut out. Cut fringes as shown in diagram. Apply the *Felton* to the inside and bottom of the tin.

Spread glue: all round the sides of the tin from top to bottom

round the edge of the base, approx $\frac{1}{2}$ in. (13 mm) wide band all round

round the inside top of the tin on the *Felton* approx $\frac{1}{2}$ in. (13 mm) wide band all round

Along gluing area of each suede side piece as shown in diagram

Stick each side piece of suede on to the tin, with each join coming at seam down the side of the tin. Start with blue suede (A) and apply so that the top edge is $1\frac{1}{2}$ in. (3·8 cm) down from top rim of tin and there is a $\frac{1}{2}$ in. (13 mm) overlap round the bottom edge. Smooth it round firmly and evenly to prevent air bubbles.

Repeat for yellow suede (B) but stick top edge $\frac{1}{2}$ in. down from the top rim of the tin. Repeat for green suede (C), but so that top edge is $\frac{1}{2}$ in. above the top rim of tin. Then turn this

over $\frac{1}{2}$ in. to the inside and press firmly down on *Felton* all round.

Turn the covered tin upside down and snip the overlapping suede all round, making cuts approx $\frac{3}{8}$ in. long. Press these firmly down on the glued area round the edge of the tin base. Spread glue all over the base and suede 'turn-over' and also over the wrong side of the blue circle. Leave for glue to dry, then press circle on to base firmly and evenly. Check that fringes are level and trim as necessary.

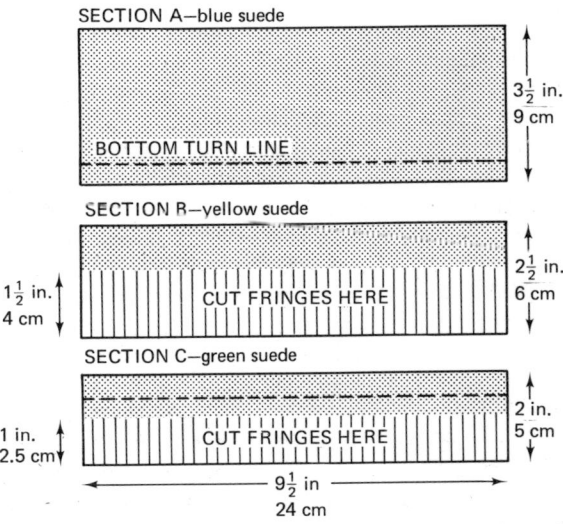

SECTION A—blue suede

$3\frac{1}{2}$ in. 9 cm

BOTTOM TURN LINE

SECTION R—yellow suede

$2\frac{1}{2}$ in. 6 cm

$1\frac{1}{2}$ in. 4 cm

CUT FRINGES HERE

SECTION C—green suede

2 in. 5 cm

1 in. 2.5 cm

CUT FRINGES HERE

$9\frac{1}{2}$ in 24 cm

63

Suede money bag

See page 77

You will need

7 in. × 12 in. (18 cm × 30 cm) yellow suede (firm quality)
2½ in. × 2½ in. (6·4 cm × 6·4 cm) red suede (any type)
Strong thread
1 yd (92 cm) fine cord for handles
Copydex
White card for pattern

To make

Draw the card up into 1 in. (2·5 cm) squares, copy the pattern on to it from the diagrams given, and cut out. Place card templates on wrong sides of suedes, mark round each piece, and cut out.

Apply glue to areas on wrong side of each main bag piece as indicated on pattern. Leave for glue to dry, then press firmly together, making sure the scallops all match.

Stitch round on line shown on pattern. Place template for motif on one side of bag, and mark all round it. Spread glue over the back of the motif and also over the area marked on bag. Leave to dry, then press motif firmly in place.

Make 2 holes approx ¼ in. (6 mm) diameter on each side of bag about 1 in. (2·5 cm) down from the top scallops. Cut the cord in half, thread one length all round top of bag through the holes, and tie ends in a tight knot on one side. Repeat with the other 18 in. (46 cm) length of cord, but tie the ends at opposite side of bag.

Lightly brush over the suede and trim any edges if necessary.

64

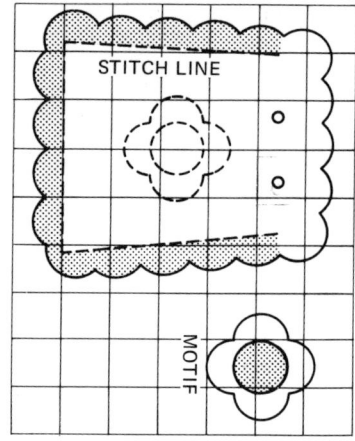

Four plait

Suede plait necklace

See page 76

This is a simple plait, using 4 narrow strands of suede and, of course, the length can be altered to suit your requirements. Make sure, though, that it is long enough to go over your head.

You will need

Approx 5 in. × 12 in. (12·5 cm × 30 cm) (or 60 sq. in.) tan suede
1 brass button with shank at back
Copydex
4 drawing pins

To make

Cut a piece of suede ¾ in. × 2 in. (19 mm × 5 cm) for tab, and leave aside. Cut 8 strips ¼ in. (6 mm) wide to start the plaiting. The length and number

Nursery waste paper bin; fringed suede pencil holder and desk tidy; shiny plastic tote bag; leather link belt

depend on the size and shape of the suede you have bought. It is simple to join in new strands — just spread *Copydex* $\frac{1}{4}$ in. (6 mm) along the end of the old strand, on the right side, leave to set, spread *Copydex* along the end of the new strand on the wrong side and leave to set, then press both glued surfaces together firmly for good adhesion.

4-plait braid (see diagram)   Use drawing pins to fasten 4 strands 4 in. (10 cm) from the ends to something stable (a pastry board is good for this) so that they are close together. Start by taking the right-hand strand and passing it over to the left, under the second strand, over the third, under the forth, and leave it there. Again take the right-hand strand and proceed as before.

Continue plaiting until braid is about 35 in. (89 cm) long, and leaving about 4 in. (10 cm) of unbraided strands. Join in new strands as necessary.

Remove drawing pins. Secure the beginning and end of the braiding with little dabs of *Copydex* to prevent unravelling.

Fold the necklace in half, right sides facing upwards, and be sure not to twist it at this stage. Glue the back of one end to the front of the other end, where the actual braiding ends, so that 8 strands about 4 in. (10 cm) long are left hanging loose for the tassel.

Tab and button   Cut a small piece of suede $\frac{3}{4}$ in. × 2 in. (19 mm × 5 cm). Using the leather side as the right side for this part, fold lengthwise into three. Make a dot in the centre of the middle section to make a little hole. Push the shank of the brass button through the hole to the back. Pass a short narrow strip of suede through the shank, and glue the ends down flat on to the tab at each side to secure the button. Spread glue all along back of tab and

also round the necklace where the braiding is secured. Leave both for a few minutes for glue to set. Then stick tab (with button) in place with the ends overlapping at the back of the work.

Lay necklace flat and trim ends of tassel to level them.

Leather link belt

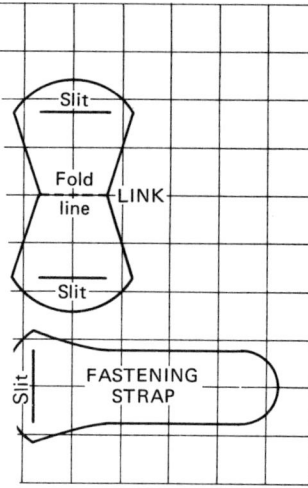

See page 65

You will need

12 in. × 18 in. (30 cm × 46 cm) piece of leather in each of three colours
3 in. × 5$\frac{1}{2}$ in. (7·6 cm × 14 cm) extra piece of leather in fastening strap colour
Brass buckle 1$\frac{1}{2}$ in. (3·8 cm) wide across the centre bar
Cardboard for templates

To make

Draw the card up into 1 in (2·5 cm) squares and copy the patterns on to it from the diagrams. Cut out both pieces. Draw round templates on to wrong side of suede and mark out links in each of the colours chosen. Cut out all links. Mark and cut out fastening strap pieces. Cut a slit at each end of each link and at one end of fastening strap as shown in diagram. Slip one of the links over centre bar of the buckle.

With the buckle front facing downwards, fold the leather link, wrong sides facing, with slots meeting. Take a second link and pass it through both slots on the first link, and fold in half meeting the slots as before.

Continue in this way until belt is desired length, making sure that the links are joined with wrong sides of leather facing on the inside.

Attach the strap link to the last link, through the slots as before. Check over each link, trimming edges if and where necessary.

Leather luggage label

See page 77

You will need

Approx $6\frac{1}{4}$ in. $\times 8\frac{1}{4}$ in. (16 cm $\times$ 21 cm) novelty-grained firm leather
$\frac{1}{2}$ in. (13 mm) brass buckle
Copydex
Strong thread
Celluloid or clear acetate
Stiff white card for name and address (also helps to stiffen label)

To make

Cut 2 pieces of leather, each 3 in. $\times$ 4 in. (7·6 cm $\times$ 10 cm). In the centre of one, draw and cut out a rectangle 2 in. $\times$ 3 in. (5 cm $\times$ 6 cm) for the front window of the label.

Glue both sections of leather together round two long and one short side, spreading just a thin line of glue round the very edge of each piece. Press firmly together to adhere. Stitch all round these three sides, about $\frac{1}{8}$ in. (3 mm) from the outer edge. Leave one end open to slot in the address card.

Cut a slot about $\frac{5}{8}$ in. (16 mm) long through both pieces of leather along the open end. Cut leather for the strap 1 in. (2·5 cm) wide and $6\frac{1}{2}$ in. (17 cm) long. Spread glue thinly over entire back. When glue has set, fold strap in half lengthways and press together firmly all along. Cut one end to a neat point and stitch all round the strap. Slide buckle on to straight end, then stitch end down on to strap. Pass pointed end through slots at end of label, ready for attaching to a suitcase. Punch 3 or 4 holes for prong of buckle to pass through.

Cut acetate to fit, and slide into place. Complete address card and slide in behind acetate.

Key ring tag

See page 76

This is a very simple tassel-type tag to make, and is suitable for almost any type of fitting.

pages 68 and 69

Brocade work bag; dolly key-holder; braided hearth brush
Velvet covered picture frame; leather dice paperweight;
ornamental shells; shell and pebble animals; framed
postage stamps; velvet covered trinket box

You will need

Key ring fitting
Scraps of leather in assorted colours
16 coloured beads, with large holes
Copydex adhesive
A length of strong thread

To make

Cut 8 strips (thongs) of leather about $\frac{1}{4}$ in. (6 mm) wide and of varied lengths from 6 in. to 10 in. (15 cm to 25 cm). Slide a bead on to each end of each thong, and tie a knot to prevent it sliding off.

Lay all the thongs flat on a table, bunched close together. Wind the thread tightly round the centre of the bunch.

Cut a strip of leather approx $\frac{1}{4}$ in. $\times$ 3 in. (6 mm $\times$ 7·6 cm). Spread glue on the wrong side of this strip, then bind it round centre of bunch of thongs (covering thread) and through the little ring on the metal fitting. Pull tightly and work round again. Glue end down firmly and secure with a few stitches.

Now cut another strip of leather about $\frac{1}{4}$ in. $\times$ 3 in. (6 mm $\times$ 7·6 cm) and spread wrong side with glue. To complete the tassel, hold bunch of beaded thongs so that they all hang downwards and bind leather strip very tightly round them all (this binding comes below and at right angles to the previous binding). Secure with a few stitches.

Suede and brass ring belt

See page 65

You will need

10 in. $\times$ 10 in. (25 cm $\times$ 25 cm) honey suede
10 in. $\times$ 10 in. (25 cm $\times$ 25 cm) tan suede
7 brass curtain rings, 1 in. (2·5 cm) diameter

9 eyelets (there are various eyelet kits available)
Giant gilt hook and eye set
Copydex
White card for pattern

To make

(each square equals 1 in. (2·5 cm))
Mark the card into 1 in. (2·5 cm) squares, copy the pattern on to it from diagram A, and cut out the card template. Place the template on wrong side of tan suede and draw round it with a pencil. Mark out 8 sections. Cut out carefully, avoiding snags along the edges. Do exactly the same for 8 honey suede sections. Spread *Copydex* all over the backs of all 16 pieces and leave for a moment or two for the glue to dry to the touch. Start joining at centre back of belt. Lay 1 tan section down with glued area facing upwards. Place a curtain ring at each end on the glued area so that the rounded ends of the suede come just past the centre of the rings (see diagram B). Place a second tan section, with the glue facing downwards, on to the first. Match round the curves and edges carefully, and press both firmly together, with the rings sandwiched between both layers of suede. Join the remaining sections in the same way, working the two colours of suede alternately. The rounded ends of each section should overlap each other a little in the centre of each ring. When you come to the front sections, attach one end to a ring and the other to a giant gilt hook and eye, with the smaller loops of these sandwiched between layers of suede.

When belt sections and rings are all joined together, mark positions for eyelets with a pencil on the suede in the centre of each ring (on the overlap). Punch holes and attach eyelets at marked positions. Follow maker's instructions when using the eyelet tool kit. The same method is used for eyelet securing hook and eye.

WORKING WITH GLUES

Introduction

Although there is a very wide variation of materials and other bits and pieces used in this chapter, adhesives are used for assembly or construction of each idea.

It would be easy to become most confused when having to make a choice of adhesive from the enormous selection available. In view of this, it is simpler to provide a little information on the glues specified in this Section.

Working with any glue can be a very messy business, so do wear an old apron, which you can keep for the purpose. The table or work surface will need protection too, even an old table. It is most annoying to find lumps of hardened glue when you start on your next project. Layers of old newspapers provide a good protection.

Copydex   This is a thick, white adhesive which is excellent for joining various fabrics, felt, leather and suede. Generally speaking, it is sufficient to apply Copydex to one surface only, and only a thin application is necessary. To prevent penetration of adhesive when joining very fine fabrics, apply *Copydex* sparingly to each surface to be joined, and leave to dry. Then press coated surfaces together for instant adhesion.

If you get *Copydex* on your hands or work surface, allow it to dry, when it can easily be peeled off. Accidental spillage on to fabrics and carpets is not so easy to remove, and will involve writing to the makers for an emergency supply of special *Copydex Remover*. They will also give information and advice on uses of their adhesive. (See page 95.)

Copydex is available in 2 oz tubes, 4 oz jars, 10 oz tins and 1 pint tins. The tubes are very practical to use, especially as a most useful little spatula comes with each tube. If you manage to collect several of these spatulas, shape the ends of one or two to points. They are then excellent for applying glue into awkward corners, or for just using a tiny amount of glue.

UHU   A clear adhesive, which dries quickly and makes strong joins. It will join together a wide variety of materials and is especially suitable for much handicraft work.

For most materials, spread a thin film of *UHU* on both surfaces to be joined. Leave a minute for glue to set, and then press both surfaces together.

UHU is supplied in tubes.

Evostik impact adhesive   This adhesive bonds powerfully on contact, after both surfaces have been covered evenly and left for 15 minutes to

pages 72 and 73

Eye of God hanging; coin rubbing picture; raffia mats
Miniature hobby donkey; fringed suede pencil holder;
large cat doorstop; covered flat iron doorstop

touch dry. It is ideal for plastic laminates, wood and metal.

Devcon 5 minute epoxy A very quick setting glue with tremendous gripping power. It bonds a great variety of hard materials, and is most useful for mending china, making jewellry and other crafts needing very strong joins. *Devcon* comes in a 2-tube pack with very good instructions and hints.

The adhesives mentioned above may be inflammable or rather strong smelling. Do use and store them in safe places away from naked flames, and allow adequate ventilation in confined spaces.

Dolly key-holder *See page 68*

You will need

4 small screw hooks
Large wooden spoon
Scraps of pink felt
Approx $\frac{1}{2}$ oz (14 g) 4-ply yellow wool
Scraps of 4-ply black wool
A few small beads and a short length of thread
UHU glue

To make

(NB when using *UHU* glue, it is advisable to apply glue to both surfaces to be joined. Leave to dry a minute or two, then press together.)

Cut a circle of pink felt approx $\frac{3}{4}$ in. (19 mm) diameter. Cut this into half for the two eyelids. Glue about 6 strands of black wool, 1 in. (2·5 cm) long, along the straight edge of each eyelid for lashes. Trim to form a curve, with maximum lash length about $\frac{1}{2}$ in. (13 mm). Glue each complete eye on to back of wooden spoon.

For the mouth, cut a 1 in. (2·5 diameter circle in pink felt. Cut in half and cut the straight edge of one half to form a 'rosebud lips' shape.

Glue in place on the face. (Discard the other half of the pink circle.)

Make the hair by cutting 21 strands of yellow wool approx 20 in. (50 cm) long. Tie the bundle of strands tightly together in the centre. Apply a little glue over and around the knot and some on the centre top of the head. Leave to set, and then press wool on to this. The strand tying the wool together forms a centre parting, but make sure the knot is glued and out of sight. Make a plait each side and tie the end to secure. Spread a little glue at each side of the face and a little on the plait, both about level with the mouth. When set, press hair against side of face to secure.

The fringe is made by winding wool several times round forefinger. Tie tightly through loops and glue in place at the front of the centre parting.

Thread the beads to a length of approx $4\frac{1}{2}$ in. (11 cm) and tie threads tightly together. Take knot round to back of face and glue very firmly inside the bowl of the spoon.

Screw one hook into the centre top of head for hanging up.

Screw one hook into the end of the spoon handle and the other two at intervals up the neck; these three hooks are to take keys.

Braided hearth brush

See page 68

You will need

Child's toy broom, approx 20 in. (50 cm) high
Approx 19 in. × 6 in. (47·5 cm × 15 cm) thick velvet to cover top
Silky fringing, enough to go round edge of brush
Approx 2 yd (184 cm) pretty braid, or enough to spiral round the handle
Evostik and *Copydex* glues

Brass ring for hanging, approx $1\frac{1}{4}$ in. ($3\cdot2$ cm) diameter

Scrap of braid to go round handle

Note These baby brooms vary in shape a great deal so it is not possible to give an exact pattern. They are available at toy shops, Woolworths and other stores.

To make

Head First measure over the top of the brush
(a) up one side, across the top, and down the other side
(b) up one end, across the top, and down the other end.
then add $\frac{1}{4}$ in. (6 mm) all round for adjustments.

Cut out a rectangle of velvet to these measurements. Mark the exact centre and cut out a neat hole, barely big enough for the broom handle to pass through. Spread a layer of *Evostik* glue all over wrong side of velvet, and leave until glue is dry and set. Spread a layer of *Evostik* glue all over the top sides and ends of broom, and leave to set. Then place velvet carefully on the head of the broom with the handle through the hole in the middle. Press velvet down very gently, easing out air bubbles. Make little tucks at the corners to ensure that the velvet fits closely and neatly. Smooth gently over for good adhesion. Trim off excess round the edges to make them level. Spread *Copydex* all along back of fringing, and also around lower edge of velvet: this band of glue must be the same width as the braid. Leave both to set, and then stick fringing in place.

Handle Spread *Evostik* glue all round and up and down the handle, including the top end. Spread glue also all along back of handle braid. Leave both to set.

Now slip the brass ring over one end of glued braid and lay this end of braid down the broom handle for about 4 in (10 cm) from the top. Press firmly for good adhesion.

Hold the handle, with the ring upright on the tip. and wind the rest of the braid spirally all down the glued handle to the base. Pull braid very tightly, and press down firmly as you work. Take the scrap of braid for handle base, glue the ends with *Copydex*, and turn under about $\frac{1}{4}$ in. (6 mm) to prevent fraying. Run a gathering thread along one edge, and draw up to fit round the handle, forming a 'rosette'. Do not join ends. Now spread *Copydex* all round the back of the rosette and round the appropriate area on the velvet surrounding the handle base. Leave both for glue to set. Then place rosette in position and press down firmly with the ends meeting closely and neatly.

Framed postage stamps

A set like this makes an attractive present for anyone. The frames measure $1\frac{3}{4}$ in. $\times 2\frac{1}{2}$ in. ($4\cdot4$ cm $\times 6\cdot3$ cm), and are available from photographic shops, gift shops and many stores at a reasonable price.

The pictures shown are Malaysian postage stamps, all of birds. Packets of modern foreign postage stamps are cheap to buy from stationers, stamp dealers and other shops, and some wonderfully colourful ones are available.

The stamps are stuck to coloured paper with a little dab of *Copydex*. Allow the glue to become touch-dry before placing them in the frames.

As well as stamps, you could frame a wide

pages 76 and 77
Suede and brass ring belt; key ring tag; suede plait necklace
Covered matchboxes; suede money bag; leather luggage label

variety of things as, for example, a miniature bunch of dried flowers (leave the glass out of the frame), sections cut from postcards, small photographs, or even pretty cuttings from magazines. All are simple and quick to make.

Nursery wall hanging

You will need

12 in. × 24 in. (30 cm × 60 cm) plain cotton or linen
5 in. × 7 in. (13 cm × 18 cm) white felt
4 in. × 5 in. (10 cm × 13 cm) brown felt
2½ in. × 4½ in. (6·4 cm × 12 cm) blue felt
4 in. × 5 in. (10 cm × 13 cm) yellow felt
3 in. × 4 in. (7·6 cm × 10 cm) pink felt
3 in. × 6 in. (7·6 cm × 15 cm) green felt
Small scraps orange felt
Small scraps black felt
Scrap of pink wool for cow's tail

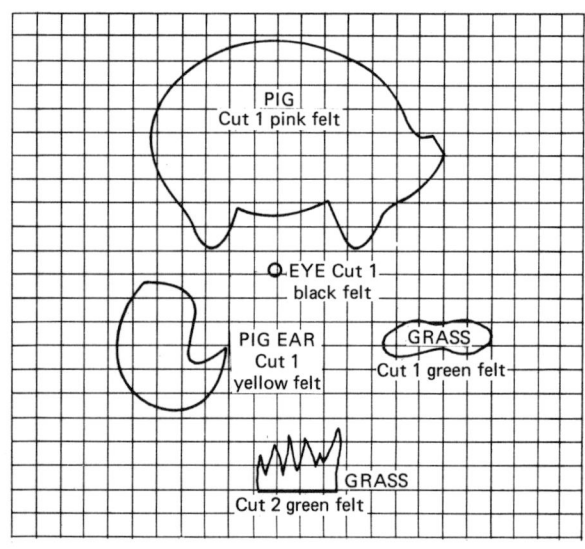

Scrap of yellow wool for pig's tail
Copydex
Sewing thread to match background
2 lengths dowel rod each 12 in. × ½ in. (30 cm × 13 mm) diameter

78

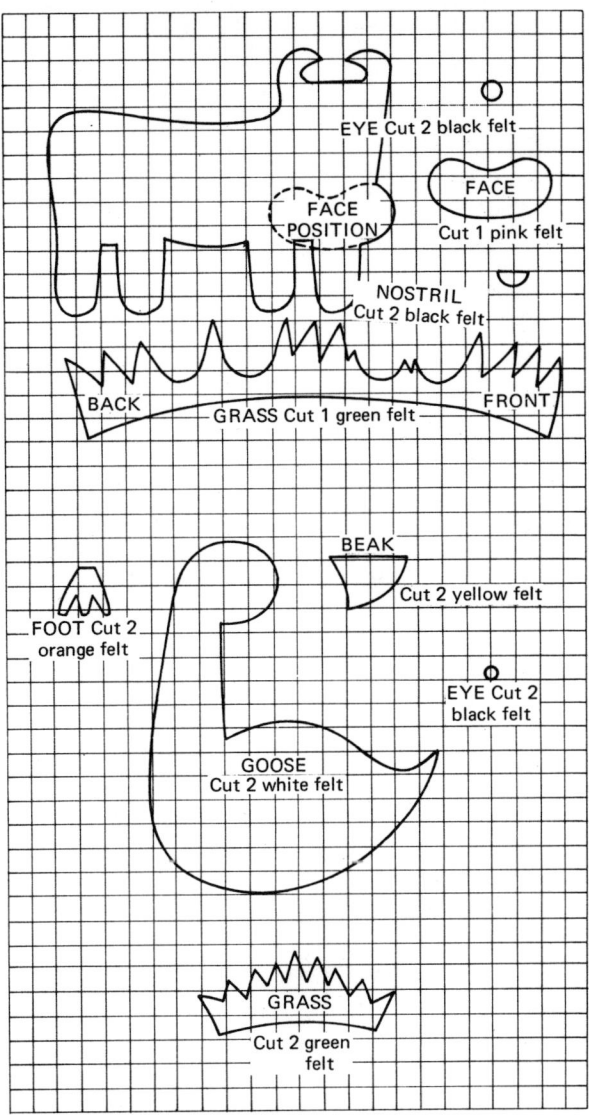

EYE Cut 2 black felt

FACE
Cut 1 pink felt

FACE POSITION

NOSTRIL
Cut 2 black felt

BACK — GRASS Cut 1 green felt — FRONT

BEAK
Cut 2 yellow felt

FOOT Cut 2
orange felt

EYE Cut 2
black felt

GOOSE
Cut 2 white felt

GRASS
Cut 2 green
felt

18 in. (46 cm) length coloured cord for hanging
Paper for pattern (or graph paper)

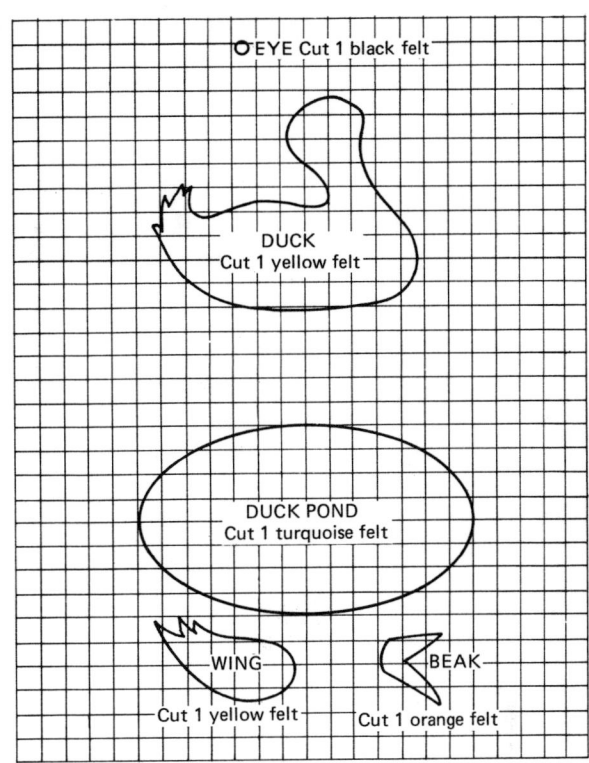

EYE Cut 1 black felt

DUCK
Cut 1 yellow felt

DUCK POND
Cut 1 turquoise felt

WING
Cut 1 yellow felt

BEAK
Cut 1 orange felt

To make

Mark the paper up into 1 in (2·5 cm) squares
and copy the patterns on to it from the diagrams
given. Cut out all pieces required. Using the
photograph of the hanging as a colour guide,
cut out all animals and features in the appropriate colours.

First spread *Copydex* carefully on the back of
the duckpond and the cow's grass, and stick
these into position. Next spread *Copydex* all
over the back of the main body piece of each
figure and glue down in place. Stick all the
smaller parts and features on after this.

'MILLE FIORI.'   Clive Hulbert. July 19

Continue until all the figures are complete and in place. Cut out tiny black felt circles for all the eyes, and tiny ovals for the cow's nostrils.

The various bits of 'grass' are made by cutting different-sized strips of green felt and snipping along one edge of each to look spiky.

Make a narrow hem along each side of the hanging. Make a hem along the top and bottom, wide enough to slide the dowel bar through. The rod should protrude from the hem about $\frac{1}{4}$ in. to $\frac{1}{2}$ in. (6 mm to 13 mm) each end. Fasten the cord to each end of the top dowel with a tight knot, leaving enough loop for hanging up.

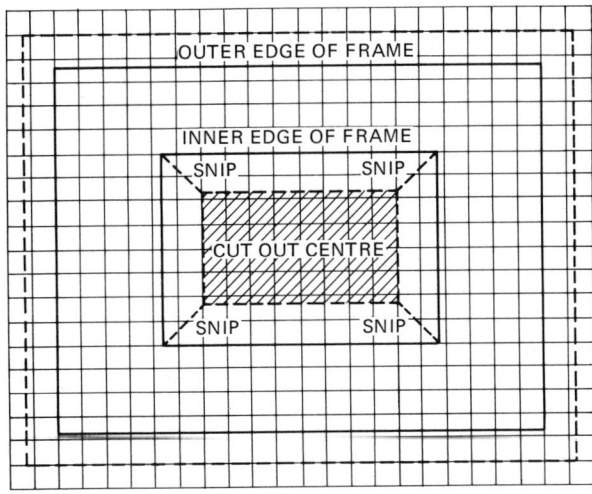

Mille Fiori – collage picture

Velvet-covered picture frame

See page 69

Most junk shops have a large number of old picture frames for sale. They can be painted gold, white, black or other colour very easily. New glass can be purchased cut-to-size quite cheaply, but make sure your measurements are correct.

This frame was a very simple one, 2 in. (5 cm) wide, covered with velvet. Gold braid is stuck round the inside edge of the frame. It is now a modern version of an old-fashioned, but very pretty, idea.

You will need

An old frame (a wide flat frame is easier to cover)
Cardboard
Evostik or UHU
Velvet, approx $5\frac{1}{2}$ in. (14 cm) bigger all round than the total area of the frame
Gold or other decorative braids to go twice round the frame
2 picture hanging rings
Hanging cord or wire

To make

Remove glass from frame and, if in good condition, wash in warm soapy water, dry thoroughly, and polish. If glass is in bad condition, buy a new piece cut to size (Builder's Merchant or Do It Yourself shop).

Remove all old tacks, nails or picture pins, and strip off any old backing paper. Wipe frame clean with a damp cloth, and leave to dry. Lay the frame front down on the wrong side of the velvet. Draw round inside and outside frame edges in pencil and cut out velvet round outside edge several inches (centimetres) out from marking line. You need enough excess

81

velvet to wrap right over and well on to the back of the frame at all edges.

Cut out centre of velvet frame about 2 in. (5 cm) towards the centre from the inside pencil line. Now snip the velvet into each corner for about 1 in (2·5 cm) (see diagram).

Spread a very thin layer of glue all over wrong side of velvet frame section, and also a thin layer of glue all over front, inside edges and outside edges of wooden frame. Leave both for a few minutes for glue to set.

Very carefully, apply the velvet to the frame. Start with the inside centre edges and pass them through front of frame to the back, and press firmly down on the narrow ledge on which the glass rests. Make the corners neat, and ease fabric round to avoid bumps. Avoid air bubbles, and keep to the marking lines as you work. Trim off extra material if necessary.

Turn the frame over, with the attached velvet, and press the velvet down gently, working each side in turn. Smooth out until it is all firmly in place, especially at the corners.

Turn frame face down and proceed in the same manner with the side edges and back of the frame. Mitre to make velvet flat and neat. Trim off excess material in the folds and at the back, if it is too bulky. Glue a line of braid all round inner edge on front of frame, and another all round outer edge.

Fit the glass in carefully, and then your picture or print, making sure that it fits snugly and cannot slide about. Cover with a layer of firm card cut to the size of the glass. Fix in place, using tiny picture pins. Tack another piece of card all over back of frame to cover all velvet edges neatly. Screw a hanging ring to each side, and attach hanging wire.

Some patience is needed for this work, but it is well worth it, especially if you match the velvet to a colour scheme.

Velvet-covered trinket box
See page 69

You will need

Small cardboard box, approx 2½ in. (6·4 cm) high and 2¾ in. (7 cm) diameter (this one is a chemist's pill box)
Scraps of velvet for sides and top
Approx 1 yd (92 cm) gold braid to trim
Various sequins and a tiny pearl bead
½ oz (14 g) *kapok*
Copydex
Note These quantities are for the box shown in the photograph. They may need to be varied to suit the box. If you can obtain a pill box, these are particularly simple to cover, and look charming.

To cover the box

(When gluing, it is important to apply it to both surfaces to be joined, and to leave until touch-dry before uniting)
Fit the lid on to the box and, with a pencil, mark round the edge of the lid on to the sides of the box. Make sure you don't stick fabric or braid above this line, otherwise the lid will not fit properly. Remove the lid. Measure round the sides and add ½ in. (13 mm) for bottom turning. Measure the height from pencil line to bottom edge, and add ¼ in. (6 mm) for turning. Cut out in velvet, with the pile running downwards.

Spread *Copydex* thinly all round sides, below pencil line, and over the lower edge just inside the rim, round the base. Leave a few moments for the glue to set.

Turn under ¼ in. (6 mm) along one short end of velvet and glue down firmly and neatly. Spread *Copydex* thinly all over wrong side of velvet, and leave to set.

When *Copydex* on box and velvet are both

dry to the touch, apply velvet band carefully round sides of box. The top edge should be about $\frac{1}{8}$ in. (3 mm) below the pencil line. Smooth all round to avoid air bubbles.

There should now be about $\frac{1}{4}$ in. (6 mm) velvet left overhanging the lower edge. Snip this all round, making each cut about $\frac{1}{8}$ in. (3 mm) deep and $\frac{1}{2}$ in. (13 mm) apart. Work round, smoothing the clipped edge firmly over and on to the base, where glue has previously been spread.

Cut a circle of felt to fit the base, and spread the back with glue. Leave to set. Spread glue all over base of box, including the turned-over velvet, and leave to set. Apply felt circle to base, and smooth over firmly.

Stick braid round the bottom of the box, and also round its side, but make sure that the upper edge of the braid does not go above the pencil guideline.

Glue sequins at regular intervals round the sides, pressing each one on very firmly.

To cover the lid

Cut a circle of felt to fit the top of the lid. Work out the arrangement for the sequins, and stitch them on. Make 3 stitches on the larger ones, and 2 on the smaller. Fasten off securely. Spread a thin line of glue all round the edge on wrong side of decorated velvet circle. Spread a thin line of glue also round inner rim of lid. When glue has set, press edges of velvet on to glued part of lid and, at the same time, insert a little *kapok* to give a cushioned effect.

Measure, cut out and glue velvet round the sides of the lid. Use same method as that for the bottom of the box, but the velvet and braid go right to the edge of the lid. The raw edges must be carefully tucked over the rim and well down out of sight. A round-ended bodkin is useful for this stage.

Brush over velvet very lightly, and neaten any edges if necessary. Turn lid so that the join meets the join on the lower part of the box.

Covered flat iron doorstop

See page 73

Old flat irons are easy to come by, there are usually plenty available in junk shops, and they can very easily be transformed into doorstops.

You will need

Flat iron (not too rusty)
Fine wire wool and medium sandpaper
Coloured enamel paint and brush
Scraps of bright-coloured velvets, braids, bobbles or other trimmings and rich materials
Felt to cover bottom of iron
UHU glue
Needle and thread to make rosette

To make

First scrub the iron in hot soapy water to remove grime, and leave to dry. Rub all over with sandpaper and then wire wool to make the surface smooth and clean. Wipe over to remove all traces of dust, etc.

Paint the ends of the handle and the side supports, and leave overnight to dry.

Place iron down on wrong side of velvet (or other fabric), mark a line round it about $\frac{1}{2}$ in. (13 mm) away from edge, and cut out on the line. Fit velvet over top of iron, between the handle supports, and cut from edge of material to supports at back and front. Then snip fabric to fit round each support (see diagram).

Spread glue all over top of iron and lightly press velvet down on to it. Apply glue round the sides of iron and lightly press down the velvet remaining from top of iron. Cut off excess fabric

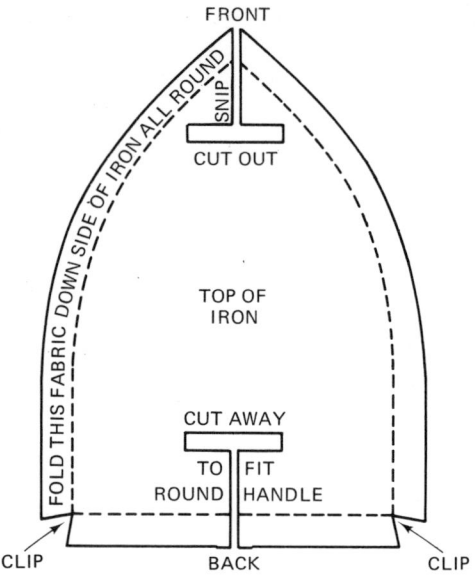

FRONT

FOLD THIS FABRIC DOWN SIDE OF IRON ALL ROUND

SNIP

CUT OUT

TOP OF
IRON

CUT AWAY

TO | FIT
ROUND | HANDLE

CLIP

BACK

CLIP

at corners, and glue down neatly. It does not matter if the velvet does not reach all the way.

Now proceed to stick braids round the sides of the iron, along the 'steps', and covering fabric joins at corners as necessary. Arrange the braids to start and finish neatly at the centre back. Apply braids round ends of handle bar.

Nearly all flat irons have the maker's name imprinted in the middle of the top. You will now see that this shows lumpily through the velvet. A rosette will disguise this prettily: run a gathering thread alone one edge of a length of braid and draw up; turn ends under, stitch together and fasten off; stick rosette over centre of iron, between the handle supports, with a bobble or small pompom in the middle.

Cut a piece of felt to fit the bottom of the iron, and glue it down. This gives a neat finish, and also prevents the doorstop sliding about on a carpeted floor.

Nursery waste paper bin

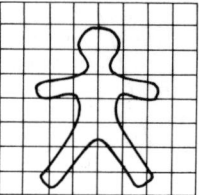

See page 65

There are so many tins, in all sorts of shapes and sizes, being thrown out. Two gallon (9 litre) ice cream tins from confectioners, or large pill tins from the chemist, both 8 in. (20 cm) in diameter, make very good waste paper bins with a little colourful 'dressing up'.

You will need

Large undented tin
White or coloured paint and brush
Approx 9 in. × 36 in. (23 cm ×   or similar
  92 cm) blue *Fablon*   self-
Approx 9 in. × 36 in. (23 cm ×   adhesive
  92 cm) red *Fablon*   plastic
7 in. × 12 in. (18 cm × 30 cm)
  white *Fablon*

To make

Wash the tin very thoroughly inside and out and leave to dry out. Apply a coat of paint to the entire inside of the tin. Paint a white band round the top outside edge, down over the 'ridge' against which the lid fitted. Leave to dry overnight. Apply a second coat of paint for a good finish and leave again to dry.

The back of *Fablon* is usefully marked into 1 in. (2·5 cm) squares. Copy the pattern of the 'little man' motif directly on to it from the diagram given. Mark and cut out 2 red and 2 white motifs. Use the first cut-out as a pattern for the other three by drawing round it on the back of the *Fablon*.

Cut a narrow band of red *Fablon* about ½ in. (13 mm) wide, and apply it round the top edge of the tin, as shown in the photograph. Peel off the backing paper gradually as you work, and smooth out air bubbles. Cut a wider band in blue (approx 7 in. (18 cm) wide according to height of tin) and apply to main area of tin. Work slowly, smoothing out air bubbles, and allow a good 1 in. (2·5 cm) overlap at the join.

Next, cut out and apply a ½ in. (13 mm) band of white plastic to the bottom edge. Now measure round the outside of the tin, divide the measurement by four, and mark a faint dot at each 'quarter point'. Peel the backing off each little man in turn and apply to blue area as shown in the photograph.

Look over the work, smooth out any air bubbles, and make sure that all edges of *Fablon* are very firmly pressed down to adhere well.

Use the left over scraps for covering little tins, or perhaps for flower motifs for drawer fronts.

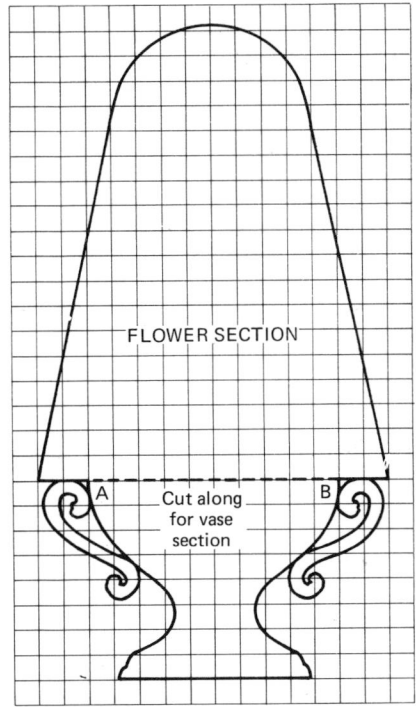

FLOWER SECTION

A   Cut along for vase section   B

Mille Fiori — collage picture

See page 80

Mille Fiori — a thousand flowers. This colourful and exciting picture is simple to make. The flowers are cut out from printed floral cotton scraps and glued in place.

It is a large picture, but equally attractive smaller ones are easily created. If you feel you cannot work out an arrangement, study pictures of flower arrangements, which will help.

General hints and reminders

Design   When choosing materials for this type of collage, decide on style of flowers and the predominant colours you wish to use. Do not mix formal, stylised flowers with informal, realistic and natural-looking flowers. Keep the same style consistent throughout the work.

Fabrics   Use firm materials which do not fray easily. Avoid thin, flimsy fabrics through which the glue might penetrate. Closely-woven furnishing cottons are ideal for this work.

Cutting   Use small, sharp-pointed scissors, and keep to the outlines of printed flowers, leaves and stalks when cutting.

Gluing   Use *Copydex*, tubes of which are conveniently provided with a tiny spatula which

85

is excellent for applying the glue to small pieces of fabric. Do not use too much glue, or it will soak through the fabric and show on the right side; only a very thin layer is necessary. After applying glue to the pieces, just hold lightly in place with the finger tips — do not press down hard. It is best to apply glue all over the back of small sections of fabric. On large areas, spread glue round the edges, adding a few smears over the central area. Avoid allowing glue to ooze out from under edges of flowers; if this happens, scrape off at once with edge of spatula provided.

To make Mille Fiori

You will need

22 in. × 32 in. (56 cm × 80 cm) natural hessian for mounting design
Scraps of furnishing cottons, printed with flower designs
9 in. × 13 in. (23 cm × 33 cm) white *Vilene* or felt for vase
Scraps of lace to trim vase
28 in. (71 cm) length of gold cord or braid
Small sharp-pointed scissors
Tape measure
Pencil and ruler
Copydex and spatula
Graph paper for patterns
Drawing pins (thumb tacks)
22 in. × 32 in. (56 cm × 80 cm) (inside measurement) picture frame
20 in. × 30 in. (50 cm × 75 cm) hardboard

Note It may not be possible to obtain exactly the same materials as used for this picture. This does not matter: the picture is just as effective made up from any scraps of furnishing cotton with largish flowers clearly printed on them.

86

VASE
Cut 1 in
vilene

Making up

Copy the patterns of the outline of the flower arrangement and the pattern for the vase on to graph paper. Cut out all in one piece. Place on hessian mounting in position as shown, and fix down firmly with drawing pins. Draw round pattern in pencil, leaving outline of work on the hessian. Remove paper. Cut off the pattern of the vase and handles separately. Cut these out in Vilene or felt, and glue in place as outlined on the hessian. Cut out several circles or other motifs from the lace, and glue along top rim of vase. Glue lines of gold trim along top edge of vase and again below the lace circles.

Cut out half circles or similar motifs from the lace and stick along bottom of vase. Apply a line of gold trim along the lower edge.

Flower application

Cut out all the coloured flowers you wish to use, and plenty of spares. Before gluing them in position, it is *most* important to lay or pin them in an arrangement 'in the vase' first. In this way you can see the whole effect, and adjust and experiment with the pieces before fixing permanently. Once they are stuck down, you cannot change them. It is best to prop the work up almost vertically to obtain the true effect of a hanging picture, and view it from a little way away from time to time while working at it.

Use the pencil outline on the hessian as your working guide. Start by gluing the flowers at the top of the picture, and gradually work downwards. To ensure a symmetrical result, work outwards from the centre of each row or layer, as well as downwards. The pencil guide must be covered by the outer edges of the flowers. Avoid the formation of too definite a line round the flower arrangement. Allow petals and leaves to jut out a little but, at the same time, keep the overall shape uniform on each side.

When you reach the top of the vase, arrange some flowers and leaves to hang over the vase, giving a soft and natural appearance to the work.

The bird perched at the bottom of the vase was a lucky find in a piece of fabric; if you cannot find something similar, a charming effect can be obtained with a flower or two instead. Position them to look as if they had fallen out of the bunch.

Finishing

Go over the work very carefully, checking that all the pieces are firmly in place. Re-glue any loose ends. Brush over the work very gently with a soft brush to remove dust or fabric fluff before framing, and trim off any frayed threads.

Framing

To preserve the picture, frame it under glass to protect from dust (and prying fingers). Before framing, make quite sure that all glue is dry and set.

This particular picture was fixed in a frame obtained from a junk shop. The edges were painted black.

Introduction

All the things in this Section are for boys and girls to make for themselves, or for each other. There are one or two presents to make for parents too. Here are a few words of advice to young creators.

Do assemble all the materials you are going to need for a particular object before you start to work.

Always read the instructions through first, so that you understand all you have to do. If there is anything you do not understand, or cannot work out, do ask an adult to explain, or to show you. It would be a pity to spoil your work for want of a little help.

Prepare a good work surface. Lay thick layers of newspaper over a table top for protection or, better still, keep a sheet of thick cardboard or even hardboard as your work top. This is easier to put away and get out again when needed.

Read the notes on page   about different glues and their uses. Be sure to replace tops of glue pots or tubes when not in use, and avoid allowing glue to get anywhere but the right place, because it can so easily ruin your work.

Do not rush through your project. Follow the instructions carefully, and carry out your work with patience. Above all, enjoy what you are doing.

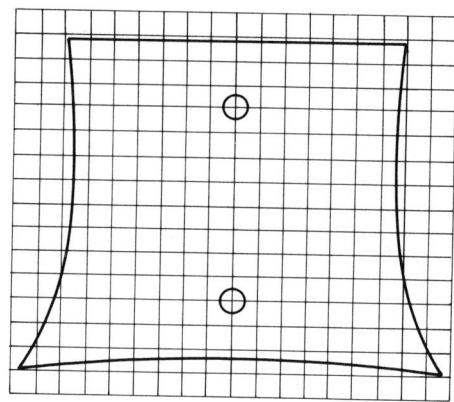

Wooden stick raft

See page 44

You will need

25 wooden sticks. (The raft in the photograph was made from 4 in. (10 cm) long matchsticks from a souvenir box bought in a gift shop. Other sticks, like cocktail sticks, standard matchsticks, etc, make a smaller but just as efficient raft. Although thicker, florists' green support canes would also be suitable
Tube of *UHU* glue
Scrap of stiff coloured paper

To make

Spread glue along one side of one stick and one side of another stick. Leave for about 5 minutes to dry, then press the two sticks together firmly.

Spread glue along one side of one of the sticks you have just joined, and then along two opposite sides of 18 more sticks. Leave for 5 minutes to dry, and then one by one stick them together. Press each one firmly against the last one, and make sure the ends are level.

Glue 4 sticks for cross bars on the underside of the raft, one near each end and the other two evenly spaced in between.

Take the last stick for the mast, and sharpen one end to a fine flat point with a penknife. Make a little slit with the point of the knife in the centre of the raft, but a little nearer to the front end. Spread glue round pointed end of mast stick, and put a little in the slit on the raft. Leave for glue to dry, then push this glued end of the mast into the slit so that it sticks out slightly underneath the raft. Leave for glue to harden.

From the coloured paper, cut out the sail and mast holes, using the diagram given, and then slip it on to the mast through the holes, with the wider part of the sail downwards.

Coin rubbing picture

See page 72

You will need

Assortment of coins of different sizes
Hard wax crayon (black shows up best)
Thin plain white paper
Thin white cardboard
Gloy or flour paste

Coloured paper for mounting (blue is used here but red looks very good)
Old picture frame (can be obtained very cheaply at a junk shop)
Brown parcel paper
Scissors
Pencil

To make

Paint the picture frame and leave to dry hard. Place a coin under thin paper and hold in place. Rub crayon to and fro across paper over coin; the pattern will quickly appear and, by rubbing fairly hard, you will obtain clear features and a sharp outline. Rub several coins on one sheet of paper. Apply glue to wrong side of piece of paper on which you have just rubbed images, and stick on to thin white card, making sure you smooth out all air bubbles.

When dry, carefully cut out round each coin and stick on to coloured mounting paper, arranging them in any pattern you like — use the picture as a guide. When you are happy with the arrangement, stick in position.

Place coin picture in frame and replace backing, or cut a new piece of backing to size and place behind picture. Cut brown paper to fit back of frame and stick on to hold mount and backing in place.

You need not fill the frame with coin rubbings all at once. As there is no glass, you will be able to add more at any time.

Raffia mats

See page 72

General hints

1   Place a rubber band round the bundle of

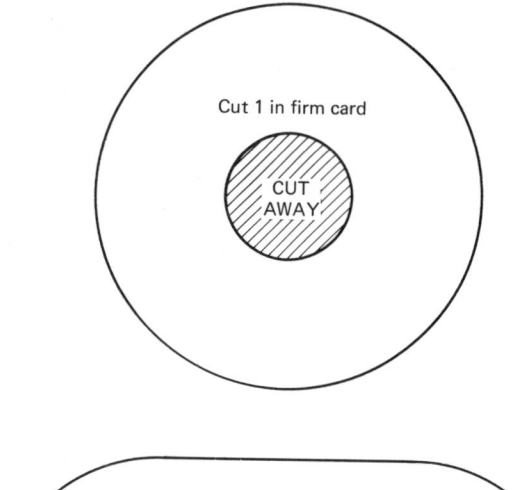

Cut 1 in firm card

CUT AWAY

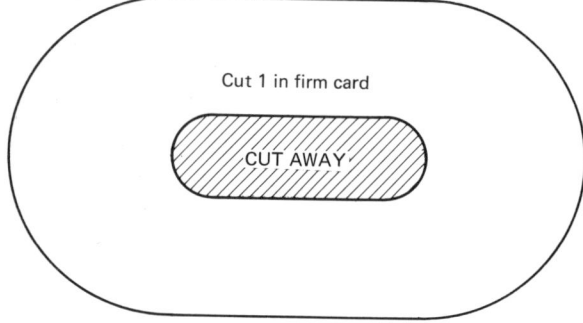

Cut 1 in firm card

CUT AWAY

You will need

Raffia or *Raffene*
Graph paper, card and paste for pattern shapes
Firm card for foundation of mats
Sellotape
The quantities of materials required will depend on the number and sizes of the mats you plan to make.

To make

(Scale: 1 square = 1 in. − 2·5 cm)
Copy the diagrams of the shapes on to the graph paper and paste on to the card, smoothing out air bubbles as you work. When paste is dry, cut out each piece. Place pattern on firm card, draw round, and cut out as many mat foundations as you require.

Winding the mats Use a small piece of *Sellotape* to attach one end of working strand to the foundation. Hold the mat with this side facing you. Take the strand over the edge, down the back, and through the centre hole to the front. Working clockwise, continue winding, overlapping each strand until the card is completely covered. The *Sellotaped* end will then be hidden. Make sure the work has the same appearance on both sides, so that the mat will be reversible.

Joining ends Use *Sellotape* again to fasten the end of the finished strand and the beginning of the new strand to the card. Make sure that the ends are covered by further winding.

Finishing ends Thread the end through a bodkin and run a little way under the wound strands. Ease the strands apart slightly. Pull off bodkin and secure end of *Raffene* to card with a little *Sellotape*. Work all mats in the same way, round and oval alike.

Raffene to avoid it coming loose and tangled.

2 It is best to flatten the strands between fingers and thumb before starting, to ensure they remain broad and flat.

3 The cardboard foundations must be completely covered. The *Raffene* strands should overlap a little round the outer edges, and then more closely round the centre hole.

4 Do not allow any knots in the work: they make unsightly knobs, and prevent the mat from lying flat on the table.

Eye of God hanging (*Ojo de Dios*)

See page 72

You will need

Approx 10 in. (25 cm) length of ½ in. (13 mm)
 thick dowelling
Scraps of coloured raffia
Feathers for trimming
UHU glue
Sandpaper

To make

Round off and make smooth each end of both
lengths of dowel rod. Place the centre of one
on the centre of the other to form a cross. Bind
them together very tightly at the centre with
raffia, as shown in the diagram. (Do *not* notch
the rods at all before joining, as the final result
will not be the same.)

Now start winding raffia round the rods,
continuing with first colour. Take it over the
next rod, round the back of this rod, round and
across the front again, and so on to the next rod
(see diagram).

The entire square is worked in this way, using
different colours, and varying the number of
rounds in each colour as you wish. The front
is the smooth side, and the 'bound rod' is the
back. You will find that the raffia strands slope
down from the 'upper level' rod to the 'lower
level' rod: this is part of the beauty of the finished
work. Always arrange joins to come at the back
of the same rod. After knotting ends together,
lay them flat against rod so that subsequent
winding will bind them down neatly.

Continue winding raffia from rod to rod until
work reaches to within ½ in. (13 mm) of each
end of each rod. Fasten off neatly at the back.
Glue down any short loose ends.

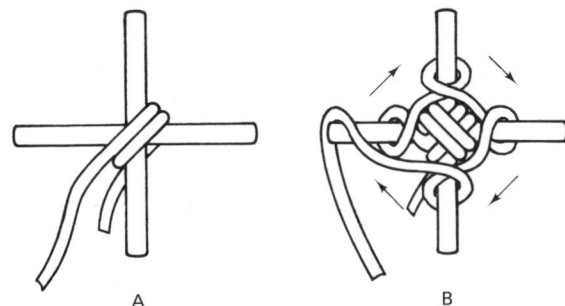

A   B

Decorate the ends of the rods. Glue several
feathers to end of each rod, then bind round
tightly with raffia. Secure end of raffia at back
of rod with a dab of glue. Tie a loop of raffia to
the top for hanging up.

Note This looks good in almost any material
which will wind easily, eg cord, wool, string,
embroidery silks, etc. Feathers, beads, tassels
of matching yarn, and other bits and pieces
make attractive trimmings. The feathers used
here were pulled out of a feather duster.

Pencil holder or desk tidy

See page 65

You will need

A round soup or fruit juice tin (of any size or
 shape you wish)
Coloured or natural cords, twines, or parcel
 string of even thickness
UHU glue
Felton (self-stick felt), to line inside of tin

To make

Remove labels from tin. Make sure that all
edges are smooth and safe.

Draw round base of tin on to paper backing of *Felton*, and cut out. Peel a little paper away from back of circle and press the sticky part in place to one side of bottom inside tin. Peel off rest of paper and press remainder of felt in place.

Measure all round inside tin, add ½ in. (13 mm) for seam overlap, and cut out *Felton* to fit. Peel backing paper away gradually, and press *Felton* in place, working carefully to avoid air bubbles.

Spread a 1 in. (2·5 cm) band of glue all round the side of the tin, at the bottom edge. Lay end of string on to the glue and wind remainder round and round tin, keeping strands very close together and making sure that the first few winds cover the starting end.

Continue up to the top of the tin, only applying a 1 in. (2·5 cm) band of glue at a time. Join in other colours to form stripes, but make sure that starting and finishing ends are well stuck down and covered by further winding.

When you reach the top, and while glue is still 'wet', pass the finishing end of the string under the last 3 or 4 turns, and pull through very firmly. Cut off end of string, very close to side, and press down well in between worked turns.

Covered matchboxes

See page 77

You will need

Standard or giant matchboxes, or book matches
Scraps of brightly-coloured wrapping paper with small designs
Gloy paste

To make

Simply cut paper to fit top and bottom of

matchbox and glue in place. Cut paper to fit the ends of the box and glue in place, or cut single motifs from the paper and glue on to each end. Smooth down well to avoid air bubbles and wrinkles.

When covering a book of matches, make sure that it opens and closes easily without tearing the paper. In some cases it may be necessary to cut the covering paper into three separate pieces for the front, back and spine.

In all cases, trim off any covering paper which overlaps edges, and re-glue any part which is not stuck down firmly.

Chicken egg cosy

See page 25

You will need

4½ in. × 9 in. (11 cm × 23 cm) yellow felt for outer cover
5 in. × 12 in. (13 cm × 30 cm) orange felt for lining and features
1½ in. × 3 in. (3·8 cm × 7·6 cm) black felt for eyes
Matching threads
Graph paper, thin card and paste for making the patterns

To make

(scale 1 square = 1 in. − 2·5 cm)

Copy all the diagrams carefully on to the graph paper, then paste on to thin card, smoothing out air bubbles as you work. When paste is dry, cut out each piece.

Place pattern pieces on to felt, draw round each one, and cut out all parts required as follows:

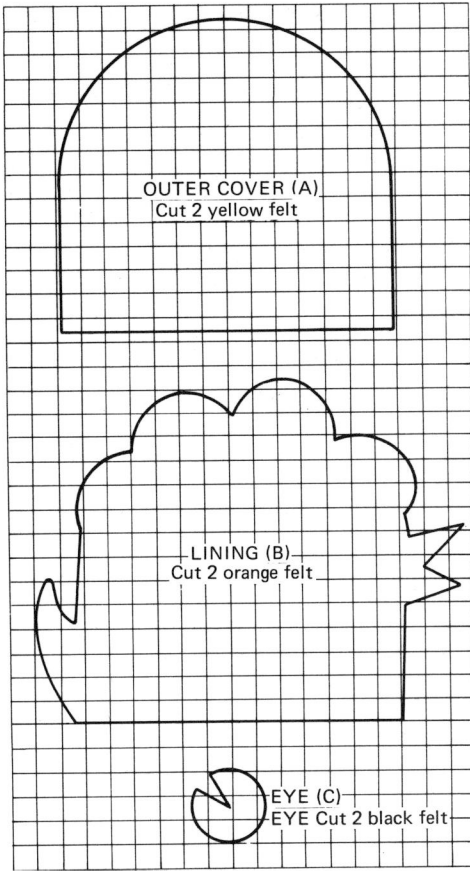

OUTER COVER (A)
Cut 2 yellow felt

LINING (B)
Cut 2 orange felt

EYE (C)
EYE Cut 2 black felt

corners. Tack together through all four thicknesses up the sides and round the top. Tack the bottom edges together, but only join one yellow edge and one orange edge.

Now use a small running or stab stitch to sew all round edge of yellow part, through two thicknesses of felt round bottom of cosy, but through four thicknesses up sides and round the top. Then stitch the protruding edges of the beak, tail and comb scallops together.

Pin an eye in place on each side of cosy and oversew round each piece.

Trim any unevenness round edges of felt if necessary.

Woolly pom-pom toys – owl

See page 17

You will need

Approx 6 oz (170 g) knitting wool (various coloured scraps may be used up)
2 circles of thin card, each 4 in. (10 cm) diameter with $1\frac{1}{2}$ in. (3·8 cm) diameter holes cut out of centre
2 circles of card, each $2\frac{1}{2}$ in. (6·3 cm) diameter with $\frac{3}{4}$ in. (2 cm) holes cut out of centre
1 in. × 3 in. (2·5 cm × 7·6 cm) white felt for eyes
1 in. × 2 in. (2·5 cm × 5 cm) black felt for pupils
$1\frac{1}{4}$ in. × 3 in. (3·1 cm × 5 cm) yellow felt for beak
2 in. × 4 in. (5 cm × 10 cm) pink felt for wings
Copydex adhesive
Graph paper for pattern

To make

Copy the pattern on to the graph paper from the diagrams given (each square = 1 in. – 2·5 cm), and cut out all pieces required. Cut out all pieces required in felt.

From yellow felt, cut 2 of piece A for outer cover
From orange felt, cut 2 of piece B for lining and features
From black felt, cut 2 of piece C for eyes
Place both orange lining pieces together; making sure that beak, tail and comb scallops are well matched. Tack all round edges to hold in place while doing the rest of the work. Place a yellow outer cover on each side of orange part, matching bottom edges and

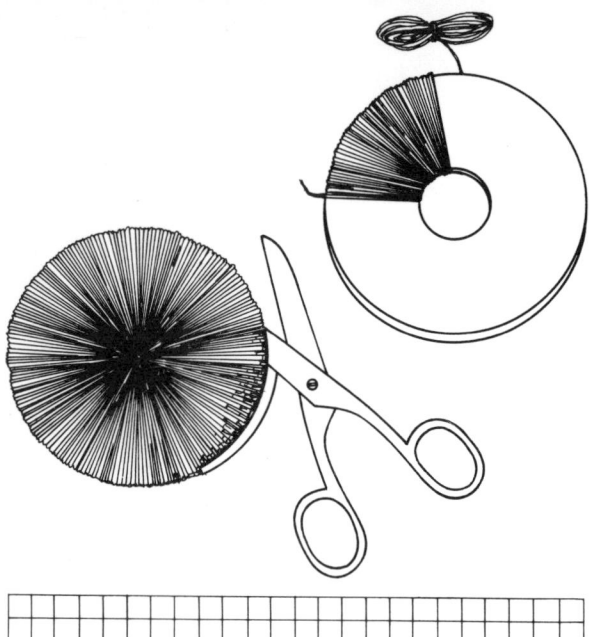

over circles and through the centre hole each time (see diagram). Keep the strands close together, and the layers of an even thickness all round. Continue winding in this way until the centre hole is filled up. You will need to use a bodkin towards the end. New wool is joined in by just laying the end of the new strand on the end of the old strand of wool.

Cut the wool strands all round the outer edge of the circle, keeping the scissor points between the two layers of card as you cut (see diagram).

Take a long length of thread and wind it three or four times round the bunch of wool at the centre and between the two card circles. Pull *very* tight to make sure that all the strands of wool are held together and cannot slip out. Leave long ends of thread hanging loose. Carefully ease off the card circles and fluff out the wool.

Body　Using the larger card circles, wind the wool and work exactly as for the head.

Join pompoms together by tying the ends of threads together, pulling the two balls very close and fastening off very tightly. The smaller ball should nestle into the larger one. A dab of *Copydex* between head and body will make a firm join.

Cut off ends of threads and trim head and body into a good shape.

Spread a thin layer of *Copydex* on the back of each felt eye white, and stick in place as shown in the photograph. Then glue the pupils on to the eye white, both facing in the same direction.

Spread a thin layer of *Copydex* along top edge of beak, and stick in position.

Spread a thin, round patch of *Copydex* at top of each wing and stick one to each side of toy, fairly high up. Hold each felt feature in place for a second or two, to make sure that they are securely attached to the toy.

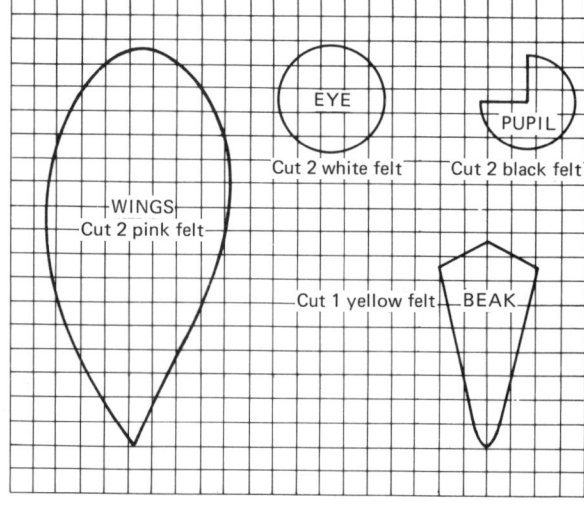

The method of making is the same for both balls (ie body and head).

Head　Place both smaller card circles together and use as one. Wind wool round and round

94

SUPPLIERS

GREAT BRITAIN

Most of the materials can be bought from large department stores or from any of the following firms:

Beads and sequins
Ells and Farrier Limited
  5 Princes Street
  London W1R 8PH
John Lewis and Co Ltd
  Oxford Street
  London W1
Sesame Ventures
  Greenham Hall
  Wellington
  Somerset

Dylon
Dylon International Limited
  London SE25 5HD
Mayborn Products Limited
  Dylon Works
  Sydenham
  London SE26

Embroidery threads and accessories
Mrs Mary Allen
  Turnditch
  Derbyshire
Art Needlework Industries Ltd
  7 St Michael's Mansions
  Ship Street
  Oxford
Craftsman's Mark Limited
  Broadlands
  Shortheath
  Farnham Surrey
J Hyslop Bathgate and Company
  Victoria Works
  Galashiels

Mace and Nairn
  89 Crane Street
  Salisbury
  Wiltshire
The Needlewoman Shop
  146 Regent Street
  London W1
Christine Riley
  53 Barclay Street
  Stonehaven
  Kincardineshire AB3 2AR
Mrs Joan L Trickett
  110 Marsden Road
  Burnley
  Lancashire

Yarns
21 Portland Street
  Taunton TA1 1UV
  Somerset

Felt
The Felt and Hessian Shop
  34 Greville Street
  London EC1

Kapok
Woolworth's branches

Leather offcuts
Department P1
  Milldale Brading Co Ltd
  5 Milldale Road
  Totley Rise
  Sheffield S17 4HR

Suede and Leather offcuts
Grainwave (Department PN)
  15 Clifton Gardens
  London N15
Homecraft (Department B)
  10A Hayes Road
  Deanshanger
  Milton Keynes

Honeywill Limited
  22a Fouberts Place
  London W1

Oasis and Styrofoam
Available from most florists

PVC
B & G Leathercloth Ltd
  71 Fairfax Road
  London NW6 4EE

Paper and Card
Fred Aldous
  The Handicrafts Centre
  37 Lever Street
  Manchester M60 1UX
F G Kettle
  127 High Holborn
  London WC1
Paperchase
  216 Tottenham Court Road
  London W1
Reeves and Sons Limited
  Lincoln Road
  Enfield
  Middlesex
George Rowney and Company
  Limited
  10 Percy Street
  London W1
Winsor and Newton Limited
  Wealdstone
  Harrow
  Middlesex and
  51 Rathbone Place
  London W1

Trimmings
Distinctive Trimmings and Co Ltd
  11 Marylebone Lane
  London W1 and
  17 Church Street
  Kensington
  London W8

Rufflette Limited
Chester Road
Manchester M15 4JD

General firms from whom a comprehensive catalogue is available:
Fred Aldous Limited
37 Lever Street
Manchester M60 1UX
E J Arnold and Son Ltd
(School Suppliers)
Butterley Street
Leeds LS10 1AX
Arts and Crafts
10 Byram Street
Huddersfield HD1 1DA
Atlas Handicrafts Limited
PO Box 27
Laurel Street
Preston
Lancashire
Bits and Bobs
46 Church Street
Twickenham
Middlesex
Crafts Unlimited
178 Kensington High Street
London W8 and
21 Macklin Street
London WC2 and
88 Bellegrove Road
Welling
Kent and
202 Bath Street
Glasgow
Dryad (Reeves) Ltd
13 Charing Cross Road
London WC2
Hobby Horse Limited
15–17 Langham Street
London SW10
Leisure Crafts Centre
2–10 Jerdan Place
London SW6 5PT

Nottingham Handcraft Limited
(School Suppliers)
Melton Road
West Bridgford
Nottingham NG2 6HD

Vilene
From most department stores

USA

Most of the materials can be bought from large department stores or from any of the following firms:

Beads
Amar Pearl and Bead Co Inc
19001 Stringway
Long Island City
New York
Hollander Bead and Novelty
Corporation
25 West 37th Street
New York
NY 10018

Embroidery threads and accessories
American Crewel Studio
Box 553 Westfield
New Jersey 07091
American Thread Corporation
90 Park Avenue
New York, NY
Appleton Brothers of London
West Main Road
Little Compton
Rhode Island 02837
Craft Yarns
PO Box 385
Pawtucket
Rhode Island 02862
F J Fawcett Co
129 South Street
Boston Massachusetts 02111

Bucky King Embroideries Unlimited
121 South Drive
Pittsburgh
Pennsylvania 15238
Lily Mills
Shelby
North Carolina 28150
The Needle's Point Studio
7013 Duncraig Court
McLean
Virginia 22101
Yarncrafts Limited
3146 M Street
North West
Washington DC

Leather
Aerolyn Fabrics Inc
380 Broadway
New York, NY

Pellon (Vilene)
From most department stores

Kapok
Woolworth's branches

Paper and card
Grumbacher
460 West 34th Street
New York, NY
The Morilla Company Inc
43 21st Street
Long Island City
New York
and
2866 West 7th Street
Los Angeles
California
Stafford-Reeves Inc
626 Greenwich Street
New York
NY 10014
Winsor and Newton Inc
555 Winsor Drive
Secaucus
New Jersey 07094